A PURIT
TO OUR DYING NATION

Edited, adapted to modern English,
with an introductory chapter and afterword
by

R. L. Hymers, Jr.
M.Div., D.Min., Th.D.

Preface by Dr. Kenneth E. Gillming,
President of the Baptist Bible Fellowship, 1998-2001

Foreword by Dr. Thomas K. Ascol,
Executive Director, Founders Ministries,
Southern Baptist Convention

Introduction by Dr. I. D. E. Thomas,
Author of *The Golden Treasury
of Puritan Quotations*

"I preach...as a dying man to dying men"
– Richard Baxter

ABOUT THE AUTHOR

R. L. Hymers, Jr. is a graduate of the California State University at Los Angeles (B.A.), Golden Gate Baptist Theological Seminary, Southern Baptist (M.Div.), San Francisco Theological Seminary, United Presbyterian (D.Min.) and Louisiana Baptist Theological Seminary, Baptist Bible Fellowship (Th.D.). He and his wife, Ileana, are the parents of twin sons, Robert Leslie III and John Wesley. Dr. Hymers worked with Southern Baptist churches for many years. He became a fundamentalist by reading the books and sermons of the late Dr. John R. Rice. Dr. Hymers is the founding pastor of the Fundamentalist Baptist Tabernacle, the only Baptist church in the civic center of Los Angeles. Known for his strong stand for Biblical inerrancy and inner-city evangelism, Dr. Hymers is an unashamed old-time fundamentalist, who earnestly contends for the faith in the tradition of J. Frank Norris, John R. Rice, Bob Jones, Sr., and "Fighting Bob" Shuler. He has been in the ministry over forty-four years.

+ +

ADDRESS AND WEBSITE

You can write to Dr. Hymers for a list of his books and tapes at

P. O. Box 15308
Los Angeles, CA 90015.

His website is at

www.rlhymersjr.com.

DISCLAIMER AND ACKNOWLEDGEMENTS

The people or sources mentioned in this book, as well as the endorsements, do not necessarily reflect the position of Dr. Hymers or the Fundamentalist Baptist Tabernacle of Los Angeles.

The author wishes to thank his colleague, Dr. Christopher Cagan, for helpful advice and for typing the manuscript of this book. He also wishes to thank Dr. Noah Hutchings and Hearthstone Publishing for putting this book into print.

+ +

A Puritan Speaks to Our Dying Nation
Copyright © 2002 by R. L. Hymers, Jr.

All rights reserved. We encourage the use of this material; however, in order to protect the contents from change, neither this book, nor any part thereof, may be reprinted in any form without written permission from the publisher, except for brief excerpts used in magazine reviews, etc.

Printed in the United States of America.

Published by:
Hearthstone Publishing, Ltd.
P. O. Box 815, Oklahoma City, OK 73101
405/789-3885   888/891-3300   FAX 405/789-6502

ISBN 1-57558-098-5

TABLE OF CONTENTS

CHAPTER	PAGE

The book is dedicated to

Kreighton L. Chan, M.D., M.Div.

My beloved physician,
and a godly deacon in our church.

PREFACE

by

Dr. Kenneth E. Gillming,
President of the
Baptist Bible Fellowship, 1998-2001

Dr. Hymers is a very educated man. He combines this with the heart of a Paul and the boldness of a Peter to beg, to insist, to love, to reason, to positively direct people to the salvation of Jesus Christ. Dr. Hymers has approached conversion from every conceivable angle, by giving us Richard Baxter in modern English.

Never have I seen anyone describe a lost man so accurately. He tells us how we thought, felt, and acted while we were lost; when we heard the Gospel, how it affected us. He shows us how inept we were before salvation and what change comes to every true believer.

This book is filled with a superabundance of Scriptures, so that a man who disagrees must disagree with God's Word and not with the preacher.

It is so refreshing when a minister doesn't hold up his finger to see which way the wind is blowing, so as not to offend anyone from the pulpit or otherwise. Dr. Hymers is not a poll-taker nor an ear-tickler. He is a good example of a faithful preacher. You must read this great book!

FOREWORD

by

Dr. Thomas K. Ascol,
Executive Director,
Founders Ministries,
Southern Baptist Convention

The Puritans were spiritual giants whose legacy has been largely ignored to our great loss. They saw clearly the necessity of applying the whole Gospel to the whole person and they had great confidence that the message of Jesus Christ, when received by faith, is the power of God to transform lives – both inwardly and outwardly. Such insight and confidence permeate Baxter's *Treatise on Conversion*.

If the Biblical understanding of salvation which is found in these pages were to be preached once again from the pulpits of our land, reformation and revival would surely come to the people of God. And Spirit-renewed churches cannot help but impact a decaying culture. God bless Dr. Hymers for making Baxter's work readily accessible to modern readers.

INTRODUCTION

By Dr. I. D. E. Thomas,
Author of *The Golden Treasury of Puritan Quotations,*
Published by Moody Press and Banner of Truth Trust

For a long time, it seemed that the Puritans had been completely forgotten in the dust-heap of history. "Dead white men," was the viewpoint of many modern critics. However, in the closing decades of the 20th century, there was a complete resurgence of interest in Puritan history, due to the influence of men like Dr. Martyn Lloyd-Jones, Iain H. Murray, and others. The Puritans are recognized again as a tour de force. In my homeland of Britain the Puritans are highly regarded, and many in the U.S.A. are also turning to them.

One of America's noted historians of the late 19th century, John Fiske, is often quoted now on the subject:

> It is not too much to say that in the seventeenth century the entire political future of mankind was staked upon the questions that were at issue in England. Had it not been for the Puritans, political liberty would probably have disappeared from the world. If ever there were men who laid down their lives in the cause of all mankind, it was the grim old Ironsides, whose watchwords were texts of Holy Writ, whose battle cries were hymns of praise.

In the 20th century, Rabbi Marc M. Tannenbaum of New York stated:

> Not to understand Puritanism is not to understand America. Like the Hebrews, the Puritans looked upon themselves as God's chosen people, comparing their New England states to those of the ancient Israelites...For both Hebrews and Puritans, God was the only true monarch.

And, lest it be forgotten, behind the Puritan politicians were the Puritan preachers. Foremost among them was Richard Baxter, often

3

referred to as "Mr. Puritan." In one sense, Baxter could be termed as a denominational isolationist, or independent. It would be difficult to categorize him as either Anglican, Episcopalian, or Presbyterian. Thomas Manton called him, "The first [greatest] preacher in England."

Baxter was certainly a busy pastor at his church in the town of Kidderminster. He counselled over eight hundred families a year, and saw amazing results. He tells us: "When I came thither first there was about one family a street that worshipped God and called on His name, and when I came away there were some streets where there was not one family...that did not so."

In addition to all this, Baxter was undoubtedly the most prolific writer of the 17th century. He wrote no fewer than 168 books, every word written with a goose-quill pen dipped in poor quality ink. He often wrote his books whilst travelling on horse-back from one preaching-point to another. Baxter had an inkwell in his saddle! And who could ever forget some of those books – *The Reformed Pastor*, *The Saints' Everlasting Rest*, *Christian Directory*, etc.

Dr. Hymers is to be praised for publishing one of Baxter's great books in modern, readable English. Be sure to read Dr. Hymers' own introduction about current America, which he calls the "Land of the Living Dead." Also, read his afterword at the end of the book. Like many of the Puritan preachers, Dr. Hymers proclaims his message without fear or favor. You may not agree with every single statement, but you will agree when he tells you that "the future does not look bright for our churches." He makes us think deeply about the spiritual condition of this nation.

Dr. Hymers has placed the whole Christian public of the 21st century deeply in his debt, by making it possible for Richard Baxter to speak to our generation. By so doing, he may live to see America experience another Great Awakening, a time of God-sent revival.

LAND OF THE LIVING DEAD

by Dr. R. L. Hymers, Jr.

"I preach as never sure to preach again,
and as a dying man to dying men."
– Richard Baxter.

My mother carried two little paperback books in her purse till the day she died. She read them over and over until the pages were tattered and falling apart. One of them was titled *The Book of Presidents* and the other, *The United States of America Reference Book* (Both by Orville V. Webster, Los Angeles: JBG Publishing, 1990, 1991 respectively). She was reading these books the night before she went into a coma. As I took them out of her purse tonight a flood of tears ran down my cheeks.

Mother was born in Panama, Oklahoma – right across the state line from Fort Smith, Arkansas. She was from the heartland, and America was always in her heart. Mine too. I learned it from her.

Tonight I took my wife to the Hollywood Bowl for an Independence Day concert and a display of fireworks. But I was unmoved by it – utterly. You must understand that this was unusual for me. I have always felt great emotion at such events. Three years ago we attended a Dodger game on the Fourth of July and my eyes filled with tears during the fireworks, as the people in the stadium sang "God Bless America" and the National Anthem. At the Dodger event the crowd was made up of young people. Few of them were white. I was deeply moved by the singing of our old patriotic songs by the Hispanics, Orientals and other races, who made up most of the throng. As they were singing I thought, "The country belongs to them now."

Spiritual Suicide

But it was different tonight. My wife and I sat in expensive seats at the Hollywood Bowl. We were surrounded by wealthy white people. Hardly anyone sang as the orchestra played those songs. We came away from the event with the sad thought that they seemed no longer able to feel the passion, tragedy, and splendor of the American experience. For them it was stale and insignificant, just a concert and a display of fireworks – nothing more.

As we walked back to our car we passed a man who was preaching on the sidewalk. The fellow in front of me, a white man about my age, yelled an obscenity at the preacher and made an ugly gesture with his finger. I looked at the faces of the people leaving the concert with us, and saw that they agreed with his crudeness. Sensing what I was feeling, my wife said, "Robert, they're reprobate." I said, "Yes, I'm afraid you're right. I think abortion has done that to them. It has destroyed whatever spark of life was left in their souls."

You cannot give consent to abortion and still be moved by the glory of American freedom.

> "We hold these truths to be self-evident, that all men are created equal; that they are endowed by their Creator with certain unalienable rights; that among these are life, liberty, and the pursuit of happiness."

If you deny those human rights to more than forty million children, the basic meaning of our nation becomes tasteless, barren, and defunct. The hearts of our people died with those children, under the abortionist's knife. They may have continued living physically, but they committed spiritual suicide by condoning this Holocaust. They live on like zombies – shuffling across the land of the living dead.

Our country is being turned over – literally – to the kids I heard singing at Dodger Stadium. They were not white, but they were moved in their hearts by things that once moved us. Now we stagger on toward the end of our civilization – while they pick up our flag. I hope they do a better job than we did.

In the aftermath of the terrorist attacks on September 11, 2001, a wave of patriotic fervor swept across the land. But it had already begun to wane by Halloween, because it was not deep seated like the patriotism of our fathers in World War II. Like most current trends, it was little more than a short-lived fad. As Andy Warhol might have put it, patriotism had its fifteen minutes of fame. (Author's note: this paragraph was added after the September 11, 2001 acts of terrorism).

The other night I heard a preacher say, "America, with all her faults, is still the greatest nation on earth." I had heard that many times. But I didn't believe him when he said it. "The greatest nation on earth?" In what way? My wife comes from the tiny country of Guatemala. Abortion is against the law there. I wonder if her country may not actually be greater in the sight of God than our blood-drenched, God-forsaken land. I wonder if it may not already be too late to save America.

> "But they mocked the messengers of God, and despised his words, and misused his prophets, until the wrath of the Lord arose against his people, till there was no remedy" (II Chronicles 36:16).

Surrounded by Hostile Pagans

Back in 1971 Leonard Ravenhill gave a strongly prophetic statement in his book, *Sodom Had No Bible*:

> Dr. Carl F. H. Henry, when editing "Christianity Today," posed the following question to some twenty leading Christian thinkers: "Sighting the final third of the Twentieth Century, what do you think it offers the church?" The answer of Dr. Elton Trueblood intrigued me, and here it is: "By the year 2000, Christians will be a conscious minority surrounded by an arrogant militant paganism" (*Sodom Had No Bible*, Bethany House Publishers, 1988, p. 13).

Ravenhill went on to say:

> For a while I chewed over that statement and swallowed it, but the result was spiritual and mental indigestion. Meditating on it a bit more, I could see that his assessment also fitted the very day in which we are now living (ibid.).

Although Trueblood took a far more liberal stand on many issues than I would, his words already had a ring of truth to them in 1971, and his prediction has been totally fulfilled since then: "By the year 2000, Christians will be a conscious minority surrounded by an arrogant militant paganism." Whatever you may think of Elton Trueblood, you must surely agree that he accurately foretold the state of society in our time. What he said troubled Leonard Ravenhill and it ought to trouble you. The future does not look bright for our churches.

Denial

But most evangelicals are not ready to acknowledge our wretched plight. They are still in a mental mode of "denial," a term which psychiatrists use to describe a dying person who is not prepared to face reality. Most of us aren't willing to accept the fact that our churches are just a gasp or two away from death. Leading Christians clutch at almost any false hope to keep from admitting the overwhelming horror of our condition.

A few Sundays ago, a well-known preacher cheerfully told us, "There's been a change under Bush. Things are looking up." This may encourage the young and the naïve – but not me. My memory is too long.

Back in 1963 I heard them say, "We have a Protestant president now. Billy Graham even led his inaugural prayer. Things will be all right now that we have a Christian like Lyndon Johnson in the White House." But it soon became apparent that Johnson was almost as morally bankrupt as Kennedy, and he led us into the quagmire of Viet Nam as well!

Then in 1968 they said, "We have a Christian president at last. He even attended a Billy Graham crusade." The newspapers showed a photograph of him standing next to Graham, his head bowed and his hands folded in prayer. Preachers all over the country were sure that Richard M. Nixon would make things right again. Then Watergate exploded! Don't get me wrong. I believe that Nixon was a gifted president who was hounded out of office by his enemies. Only in the future will a new generation reevaluate him as a better man than the liberals made him out to be. But those preachers were wrong in 1968 when they said he would make things right. Richard Nixon did not save us.

Again in 1976 I heard them say, "Jimmy Carter is a *real* born again Christian. He's a Southern Baptist deacon, teaches Sunday School, and reads his Bible every day, you know. Things will be fine now." Then double-digit inflation hit, and the hostages were locked up in Iran! Carter presided over the most inept maladministration of modern times.

But there was no stopping them. Their bright and brainless predictions went right on in 1981. One of them went so far as to say, "With Carter there was no hope. With Reagan there is hope."

I sat with Francis Schaeffer in his living room the morning Ronald Reagan became president. But Dr. Schaeffer was far too wise to say anything breezy and positive as we watched the inauguration on television. And by this time I myself had been disillusioned enough times to stop putting my hopes in anyone at the White House – even Reagan. This good man's moment came – and went. America was not "turned around." No revival or "spiritual revolution" took place. The years dragged on, and soon Bill Clinton occupied the White House.

None of these "Christian" leaders did America the slightest bit of good morally or spiritually. If you think I'm being too negative, ask yourself – are we better off than we were forty years ago? Or are we worse off?

The other Sunday night I was skeptical when that lighthearted preacher told us, "George W. Bush is President now. Things are looking up." I thought to myself, "Bush only won by a handful of votes. We aren't even certain he can hold on to the Presidency four years from now, much less 'save' the nation!"

The idea that the President can change things is "denial" – a terminally sick nation grasping at a fanciful dream to keep from admitting the awful truth – our way of life is ending – right now!

The Third World Takes Over

Over forty million children have been exterminated since abortion became legal in 1973. Our country has been overrun with aliens as a result. *Time* magazine has a cover story titled, "*Welcome to Amexia:* The border is vanishing before our eyes, creating a new world for all of us" (*Time*, June 11, 2001). *You simply cannot kill off forty million children without somebody coming to take their place in the work force a few years later.*

Time went on to say that "Hispanics are the largest minority group in the U.S., transforming cities large and small" (ibid., p. 47). A map accompanying this article shows that they are taking over America. The map gives the percentages of Hispanics now living in several of our cities:

Los Angeles has 47%.
New York has 27%.
Chicago has 26%.
Dallas-Fort Worth has 36%.
Dodge City, Kansas has 43%.
Dalton, Georgia has 40%.
St. James, Minnesota has 24%.
Rupert, Idaho has 35%.
The Hawaiian Islands have 10%.

From coast to coast, and in the islands of the sea, another culture is replacing the Americans who were killed off by abortion. Don't get me wrong. I'm not against the Hispanics! As I said, my own wife is from Guatemala. I'm simply giving you the facts. Norman Rockwell's America is gone. The **Dallas Morning News** reports that the State of Texas will be over 50% non-white within four years (May 14, 2001, p. 1).

My wife was driving our teen-age boys through Beverly Hills this morning. They pulled up beside a classic Rolls Royce and saw TV personality Jay Leno in the driver's seat. They also noticed there weren't any other white or black people in sight. My wife said it looked like a street in Mexico, filled with Hispanic workers.

This is Beverly Hills – home of the movie stars! By creating a "minefield" of absolute contraception, and aborting any baby that happens to "make it" through alive, these people have virtually sterilized themselves, and are in the process of turning over their burned out city to a more fertile civilization.

A Cultural Death Wish

At the same time that we are experiencing this influx of immigrants, our own traditional families are disappearing. The **Washington Post** reports, "Married-with-children Still Fading. Census Finds Americans Living Alone in 25% of Households" (May 15, 2001, p. 1).

What do these figures mean? Very simply, they show that black and white Americans have stopped having enough children to maintain our way of life. The country is being overrun by people who tend not to have abortions or use contraceptives on the scale we do. This trend is also happening in the United Kingdom and in Europe.

In the *very near* future our culture will be dominated by people from another background, with another language. White Americans will age, and our nation will no longer be led by them.

The *Christian News* reports:

> By 2025 half of the American population will be of Hispanic descent. They don't believe in abortion, at least not at the rate at which the white European middle class has accepted it...*The future of this country belongs to them.* It's just that my children, and particularly my grandchildren, will be a minority in America...Life belongs to those who want to live and to those whose children will follow them (Jack Cascione, *Christian News*, January 31, 2000, p. 15).

When America ceases to have a white majority in about 2025 several things will happen. Medicare, MediCal, Social Security, and other benefits will dry up or be overturned by the new majority in the voting booths. Those who replace us will say, "Why should *we* pay the bills for those old white Americans?" *The "Boomer" generation is in for a rude awakening. No Medicare. No MediCal. No Social Security check.*

As a result of our cultural "death wish," these aging Hippies face a very dangerous and uncertain old age.

You simply cannot abort forty million children and still expect them to be here to pay your bills when you want to retire. And you can't expect the new alien majority to support you either. You sowed the extermination of forty million babies and you will reap poverty and terror in your old age as a result. They won't be here to take care of you! "Whatsoever a man soweth, that shall he also reap" (Galatians 6:7).

Will the Mormons or the Muslims Take Over?

Did you know that Mormons "eat" one Baptist church every week in the State of Texas alone? Yes, they take in about three hundred Baptists a week there. At their current growth rate they will pass the Southern Baptist Convention and become the largest non-

Catholic group in America within twenty-five years. *Calvary Contender* reports,

> **Mormons Make Converts From Baptists.** Mormons claim that they have more converts from Baptists than anybody else (May 15, 2001, p. 2).

SBC President Paige Patterson agreed that "it could be true" (ibid.). All across the U.S. the Mormons are after us.

They aren't the only ones. With the terrorist attack on the World Trade Center and the Pentagon, America abruptly entered what will probably be a very long war with militant Islam. Columnist Don Feder says, "Wherever Islam seeks to advance by force, it must be resisted...America is caught up in a world war" (Don Feder, townhall.com, September 14, 2001, p. 2). Do we have the will to win a prolonged war like this? I have my doubts.

I can picture our burned-out civilization replaced by the strident forces of Allah. "They said that if we didn't convert to their religion, they would cut our throats," one girl reported (Feder, ibid). That's pretty strong stuff for a culture like ours, that gets its ideas about religion from Oprah Winfrey and Homer Simpson, and its morality from Howard Stern and Jerry Springer. Who can say whether Islam will defeat and dominate our culture some day? (Author's note: these two paragraphs were added after the September 11, 2001 acts of terrorism).

Tonight I noticed a striking title as I browsed through a bookstore in Burbank, California. It was called *Our Emptying Churches*. Dr. James Dobson, of Focus on the Family, compares the church to the Titanic. "It is large, elegant, and sinking fast" (*Focus on the Family Newsletter*, August 1998, p. 2). Dr. Woodrow Kroll, director of Back to the Bible, states that "Between 3,500 and 4,000 churches close their doors each year in the USA. In 1900, 66 percent of the American population belonged to Bible-believing soul-winning churches...Yet it is predicted that [in a few years] there will be only 33 percent of the American population who belong to a church" (Woodrow Kroll, *The Vanishing Ministry*, Kregel Publications, 1991, pp. 31-33). The percentage of people attending conservative churches was cut by half in the 20th century.

Leonard Ravenhill came to our country from England, but he understood the problem in our churches. He laid much of the blame for their weakness on worldly preachers:

> A worldly clergyman is a fool above all fools, a madman above all madmen! Such vile, infamous wretches as these are the real ground of the contempt of the clergy. Indolent clergymen, money-loving clergymen, praise-loving clergymen, preferment-seeking clergymen – these are the wretches that cause clergymen in general to be contemned. Worldly clergymen are the pests of the Christian world, the grand nuisance of mankind, a stink in the nostrils of God (Leonard Ravenhill, *Sodom Had No Bible*, Bethany House, 10th printing, 1988, p. 120).

The churches are powerless to help our crumbling society because too many of them are led by ministers who are so worldly that they don't seek the true conversion of their members. Our decaying churches are filled with lost people as a result.

Back in the 1940s Bob Jones, Sr. estimated that 50% of church people were lost. Dr. W. A. Criswell felt that 75% of the members of his church were unsaved. A. W. Tozer and Southern Baptist consultant Jim Elliff gave an even gloomier picture. Both of these men said that 90% of evangelical church members are unconverted (see *The Church That Will Be Left Behind* by R. L. Hymers, Jr., Hearthstone, 2001, p. 3).

"Flabby Christianity"

Why has this dismal situation occurred? *Simply because many of our leading pastors are too worldly to care.* They bring junk music into their churches. They preach fifteen-minute "motivational" messages. They close the Sunday evening services. They allow their young people to come to church dressed like the neo-cretans in our failing culture. They have even brought dancing into many so-called "fundamental" churches. What's next? Anything goes – simply because these "big" preachers *don't care about the souls of their people.*

Oh, I know the arguments these pastors use. I know they are reacting to the Phariseeism and hypocrisy they saw when they were

13

young. But they have rebelled the wrong way. Instead of seeking the reality of God, they have turned to the lust of the flesh, the lust of the eyes, and the pride of life. Instead of turning from Phariseeism to God, they have turned to the world, the flesh, and the Devil. They have poisoned our churches instead of getting our people truly converted. As Dr. Tozer put it, they preach sermons that contain a

> flabby Christianity, intellectually impoverished, dull, repetitious [that] to a great many persons are just plain boring. This is peddled as the very faith of our fathers in direct lineal descent from Christ and the Apostles. We spoon-feed this insipid pablum to our inquiring youth and, *to make it palatable, spice it up with carnal amusements filched from the unbelieving world. It is easier to entertain than to instruct, it is easier to follow degenerate public taste than to think for oneself, so too many of our evangelical leaders let their minds atrophy while they keep their fingers nimble operating religious gimmicks to bring in the curious crowd* (A. W. Tozer, *The Set of the Sail*, Christian Publications, 1986, pp. 67-68).

The Pests of the Christian World

What is the motive behind this kind of ministry? The answer is simple enough. These "progressive" preachers are in the main men who have never been converted. Most of them were "church kids" who grew up in the stuffy mildew of a dying religion. They raised their hands or came forward at "invitation time." They were instantly pronounced "saved" and baptized into the fellowship of the church. They grew up snickering in the pews, passing notes, and telling off-colored jokes after Sunday School. Some of these "church kids" were then manipulated into going to Bible school or seminary, where they were taught to manipulate others, the way they themselves had been manipulated. As a result, these unconverted "church kids" now lead most of the larger congregations in our nation into every hare-brained scheme of human manipulation that comes along. You name it: vapid music, insipid Bible versions, mawkish preaching and "touchy-feely" professionalism on the one hand – and Ruckmanism, incompetent evangelism, and cold Phariseeism on the other. The "church kids" of the sixties and seventies are taking over our pulpits – and *killing our churches*. As Ravenhill said, these "clergymen are the pests of the

Christian world, the grand nuisance of mankind, a stink in the nostrils of God."

We need something better than what they offer us with their dry-as-dust "expository sermons," with hackneyed ideas culled from the modern writings of a few shallow authors. We need something better than their superficial form of evangelism and refusal to personally counsel the lost. *I say that we need something better than these Philistines have given us!*

But where can we look to find better examples and better models for ministry? *I say we should look to the Puritans!* These preachers paved the way for the First Great Awakening – and the Second Great Awakening – and the Third Great Awakening! And if we hope to have a real revival in our day, it is to the *Puritans* that we must look once again.

And there is no better place to start than with Richard Baxter, the most prolific writer and preacher of all the Puritans. I believe that the writings of Baxter are exactly what we need in our churches today. Let me tell you about this man who was highly regarded by George Whitefield, John Wesley, C. H. Spurgeon, Martyn Lloyd-Jones, and a host of others.

Richard Baxter's Message

The best known of the Puritan preachers is Richard Baxter (1615-1691). He has been called "the most successful preacher, winner of souls, and nurturer of souls that England has ever had." Edmund Calamy called him "The most voluminous theological writer in the English language." Baxter wrote over 160 books.

Born in Shropshire into a somewhat poor family, he never attended a university and was always physically weak. Yet he acquired great learning on his own. He became the pastor in Kidderminster, a town near Birmingham, in 1647. The people who lived there were very wicked when he came. The pastor he replaced was a drunkard, who preached only once every three months! Hardly any of the church members were converted when his ministry began. During his years at Kidderminster he visited each person individually every year, among the 800 families in his church. He taught his people one-by-one. Baxter wrote about his method of pastoring in his famous book, *The Reformed Pastor*. John Wesley thought so highly

15

of this book that he recommended it to his Methodist preachers. I believe it to be the greatest book on pastoring which has ever been written.

Baxter sought to mediate between Arminianism and Calvinism by advocating a form of free will, through grace. He believed that his method was a middle way, which he called "mere Christianity" (in the twentieth century C. S. Lewis used Baxter's phrase as the title of one of his popular books).

Baxter's great strength lay in his evangelistic preaching and his pastoral ability. The main purpose of his sermons was to see the lost converted. His book, *A Call to the Unconverted*, is a hard-hitting plea for the lost to come to Christ. The outstanding feature of his preaching was his earnest zeal. In both his writing and his sermons he put forth his belief that preachers need "the skill necessary to make plain the truth, to convince the hearers...to screw truth into their minds and work Christ into their affections."

Although he preached in Westminster Abbey, before the King, and before Parliament, his favorite pulpit was in his own church, speaking to the poor people of Kidderminster.

He was put in prison in the Tower of London for eighteen months, rather than submit to the Church of England, after the Act of Uniformity was passed. He was often visited while in prison by the famed Bible commentator Matthew Henry.

Baxter's *Treatise on Conversion* was written in 1657. It is a wonderful book, but the wording is too lengthy and complicated for most readers today. I have condensed it, rearranged some chapters, and changed difficult words to simple ones, to reach the less literate mind of modern man. I have tried my best to convey the basic ideas Baxter presented in the original book in an interesting and readable way. I hope it is a blessing to you. It corrects the shallow preaching of "decisionism" which has overthrown true evangelism in our time.

Before you dismiss a book written back in 1657, remember these words from Winston Churchill:

> "The farther backward you can look, the farther forward
> you are likely to see."

Most current religious writers repeat each other's ideas with no input from an objective source. Baxter is a voice from outside the "system" – a ray of light that penetrates the social vacuum, and shatters the stereotypical assumptions of the arrogant snobs who palm themselves off as the new and progressive leaders of evangelicalism, but who actually offer only hackneyed platitudes. In stark contrast, Baxter's thoughts are so old that they spring from the page with newness of life. His message is exactly what our churches and our nation need.

I love America with all my heart. My father's father and grandfather came here from England for a better life than they had slaving in a mine shaft in Cumbria. My mother's people were flag-waving patriots from the heartland, who instilled in me a deep love for our nation which has never faded. People who know me best can tell you that there is not the slightest pretense or artificiality in this chapter. Nothing was said for "effect." *I believe what I have written in the very marrow of my bones.*

As I sit here alone tonight, with tears streaming down my face, I beg you – in the name of God – pay attention to Richard Baxter! Let him speak to our dying nation!

R. L. Hymers, Jr.
The Pastor's Study
July 4, 2001

17

"Not until all is lost will many awake to the painful reality that America as we once knew it is gone"
— Dr. Erwin Lutzer,
Pastor of the Moody Memorial Church.

"Savages are stirring the dust of a decadent civilization, and already slink in the shadows of a disabled church"
— Dr. Carl F. H. Henry,
evangelical theologian.

"Civilization based on a Judeo-Christian foundation has collapsed. In its place the West without exception now lives and functions as a pagan world"
— Dr. Harold Lindsell,
editor-emeritus of *Christianity Today*.

"I am not a religious man, but America is now in moral anarchy. I do not believe it can even survive without a sweeping spiritual revival"
— Judge Robert H. Bork,
rejected Reagan nominee to the Supreme Court.

A TREATISE
ON CONVERSION

by

Richard Baxter

A.D. 1657

"I preach as never sure to preach again,
and as a dying man to dying men."

Edited and adapted
to modern English by

R. L. Hymers, Jr.
M.Div., D.Min., Th.D.

CHAPTER ONE

MISERIES OF THE UNCONVERTED

"Destruction and misery are in their
ways" (Romans 3:16).

Great numbers of people in the world have never been
converted, yet they live as though everything were all right with
them! If you ask twenty of them whether they are converted, some
will say they hope so, but are not sure. Some will make fun of you or
be angry with you for asking. Most won't even know what
conversion is, although the Bible plainly says that a person must be
converted to enter the kingdom of heaven.

Suppose someone asked you if you're converted. What would
your answer be? Are you *absolutely certain* that you have
experienced it? Have you ever asked yourself, "What will happen to
me if I am not converted?" May you be awakened to your need by
the following points.

1. *As long as you remain unconverted, you are not a true
   child of God, or a real Christian, because you do not
   truly know Jesus Christ.* Therefore, you cannot say
   that God is your Father. You are not His child. In fact,
   you are still His enemy. Your heart is concerned only
   with earthly things.

   The whole world is divided into two classes of people,
   the children of God and the children of the Devil. Only
   those who are converted are the children of God (John
   1:11-12; Romans 8:9). Everyone who is unconverted is
   a child of the Devil, as Christ Himself told us (John
   8:44). The Bible says, "In this the children of God are
   manifest, and the children of the devil" (I John 3:10). It
   is only by saving faith in Christ that you can be made a
   son or daughter of God (Galatians 3:26; Ephesians

3:17). Those who are unconverted do not have saving faith in Christ.

When you pray, you cannot have comfort because God is not your Father. It is conversion that turns your heart to God, and if He does not have your heart, you are not His child. None of the unconverted are His children. You may call God your Father as much as you like, but He will never agree with you until you are converted. You may call Him "Lord, Lord" until you die, but He will tell you that He does not know you (Matthew 7:22).

By nature you are in a different class from those who are converted. This is the very essence of true conversion. You must be humbled and broken off from trusting yourself and all others, so you can be planted in Jesus Christ, the living vine. No matter what you say, you are still only a dead branch, and you will be gathered up and burned in the fire (John 15:1, 4-6). You can't be a human without being born. And you can't be a Christian without being born again. The union of Christ and true Christians is in the heart. Words and prayers will not unite your heart to Jesus Christ.

2. *Think farther, there is no hope of salvation for any lost person who lives and dies in an unconverted state.* This is true whether you like it or not. If this offends you, I can't help it. You are offended by the words of Christ. Even if you think that this is a hard saying, it is still a true one, because Christ cannot lie. Remember that He said:

> "Except ye be converted, and become as little children, ye shall not enter into the kingdom of heaven" (Matthew 18:3).

When you read that verse, you may refuse to believe it. What a hypocrite you are if you say you're a Christian, but you don't believe the words of Jesus Christ!

21

What will you get by not believing? It will only lead you to more self-delusion and ruin. If you don't believe Christ, how can I expect you to believe me? Some day soon Christ will say, "Bind him hand and foot...and cast him into outer darkness" (Matthew 22:13). Then you will weep and gnash your teeth.

If you can't believe Christ, then you can't believe anybody! But if you do have confidence in Christ, then you must believe that no unconverted person can enter the kingdom of heaven. Don't be so foolish as to think these words are mine. They are the words of Jesus Christ Himself.

> "Except ye be converted, and become as little children, ye shall not enter into the kingdom of heaven" (Matthew 18:3).

If Satan and sin have hardened your heart so much that you will not believe, you will not enter the kingdom of heaven. You will remember His words whether you want to or not at the Last Judgment.

3. *Think even farther – while you remain unconverted you can't have any of your sins pardoned.* All the sins you have ever committed condemn you. You will answer for every transgression before God. You will suffer as a result of your sins for all eternity if you remain unconverted. When Christ told us about those who committed the unpardonable sin, because they resisted His converting grace, He said, "Lest at any time they should be converted, *and their sins should be forgiven them"* (Mark 4:12). This shows your sins are not forgiven unless you are converted.

Think how awful it is to have a whole load of unforgiven sins on your record. Only one unforgiven sin will condemn you forever, just as one stab in the heart will kill a person. What then will happen to you if you have thousands of unforgiven sins? You surely have countless sins on your record, don't you? What will happen to you when these sins are judged by God?

An unforgiven sinner is lost just as surely as the demons themselves are lost. In fact, *you are lost.* Christ tells you what will happen to you after you die. He will say to you,

> "Depart from me, ye cursed, into everlasting fire, prepared for the devil and his angels" (Matthew 25:41).

> "There remaineth no more sacrifice for sins, but a certain fearful looking for of judgment and fiery indignation, which shall devour the adversaries" (Hebrews 10:26-27).

How horrible it's going to be when you stand before the throne of God with unforgiven sin on your record. God's judgment for these sins will be heavier on your soul than a mountain upon your body, and will push you down to everlasting torment. Unforgiven sin is the very fuel of Hell.

You cannot be saved after you die. It is everlastingly too late then. You must be converted now, while you are still alive, or you will spend eternity in torments. I did not make up this doctrine. It is taught throughout the Bible. You will say, "Lord, Lord, open to us." But Christ will say, "I know you not" (Matthew 25:11-12). He will then say, "I never knew you: depart from me, ye that work iniquity." These are Christ's own words (Matthew 7:21-23).

If you hope to go to Heaven, and not be sent into everlasting misery, you must search for Christ now. Only Christ can pardon your sins. No one ever obtained pardon after death.

What I'm telling you is the same thing that Peter preached:

23

> "Repent ye therefore, and be converted, that your
> sins may be blotted out..." (Acts 3:19).

I hope you will pay close attention to those words. That
verse shows that no one's sins are blotted out unless he
is converted.

4. **The next thing I want you to think about is this: As
long as you are unconverted, you are a slave of Satan.**
You are under the Devil's power, and are led about as
his captive. You may not think this is true, but it is
anyway. God's Word says so. Until a person is
converted he remains a captive, a slave of Satan. Only
when you are converted will you escape from slavery
and become free – a son or daughter of God.

> "He that committeth sin is of the devil...In this the
> children of God are manifest, and the children of
> the devil..." (I John 3:8-10).

This verse tells us that the person who gives himself to
sin belongs to the Devil; and he who gives himself to
Christ is a child of God.

The Devil is the one who makes you hate the thought of
conversion. It is Satan who makes you think you are
converted already. It is him who tells you that you have
plenty of time and not to worry about getting saved.
The Bible tells us that this is Satan's work, which Christ
came to destroy (I John 3:8).

If a man is put in prison and placed in a dark dungeon,
he will certainly cry out, "Oh, I wish I were free!" You
could be free. You could be delivered from Satan. But
you are not willing! Christ has provided His Blood to
wash away your sin. But you don't want it. God
"would have all men to be saved, and come to the
knowledge of the truth," but most people do not want to
be saved. They would rather remain the slaves of
Satan. Remember this: all people are the Devil's slaves

until they are converted. If you do not want to live and die as his slave, don't put off your conversion any longer.

5. *Another misery is that nothing you do will truly please God as long as you are unconverted.* Prayer, church attendance, Bible reading, giving your money, witnessing – none of these things please God at all if you are not converted. God is displeased with the very best works performed by an unconverted person.

> "He that turneth away his ear from hearing the law, even his prayer shall be abomination" (Proverbs 28:9).

Unconverted sinners do not realize that their prayers and church attendance, and other religious duties are actually hated by God.

> "Ye are they which justify yourselves before men; but God knoweth your hearts" (Luke 16:15).

> "Thou hatest all workers of iniquity" (Psalm 5:5).

> "Every one that is proud in heart is an abomination to the Lord" (Proverbs 16:5).

Please don't think that I'm telling you not to pray, or read the Bible, or go to church. I am certainly *not* telling you to stop doing those things. They will be the means God uses to convert you. But I am saying that the mere repetition of these duties will not help you any more than they helped the Pharisees in the time of Christ. You must withdraw from the deceitfulness of sin and stop resisting the grace of God. Come fully to Jesus Christ and be converted. Nothing you do can truly please God until this happens to you.

> "So then they that are in the flesh cannot please God" (Romans 8:8).

Only a converted person can ever be pleasing to God.

6. *Another torment of unconverted persons is that they live in continual danger of damnation.* Although God has patiently held back His judgment so far, you live in *continual danger of damnation* if you are unconverted. You live constantly under the wrath of God. You are under the curse of the law at all times. You do not know when judgment will fall on you. No unconverted person can tell how long he will live in this world. Judgment and death could come at any moment. A person who is going to Hell does not know if it will happen today. Such people, if they are thinking at all, can never feel peace or security.

Every second you are living at the very edge of Hell! You may fall into it at any time. *You may be in Hell one hour from now!* Every morning when you get up, and every night when you lie down, you are never sure whether you will be in Hell the next day.

Many dying people have been terrified when they thought that in a few minutes they would be among demons in the fire of Hell! What a hideous thought! What a terrible fear! How horrible to have demons clawing at you, to be sucked under and gnawed upon by the worm that dieth not, to be burned horribly again and again, without any relief, to be tormented with painful thirst night and day!

Let the thought of this give you no rest until you are truly converted. Until then, you can never be sure of safety. *You are in continual danger at all times!*

7. *There is another horrible thing for unconverted people – they have no basis for even one hour of peace!* How can a person be happy who is in such a condition as this? *If your eyes were open, you would either be frightened out of your sins or out of your mind! If these things became real to you, you would either be frightened into conversion or into insanity!*

26

Dr. Hymers' note: This is similar to what happens in suicide, which is much like conversion – but without grace. In suicide, the mind sees the hopelessness of life. There is no rest, night or day, in this state of hopeless depression. So, the person commits suicide. In conversion, the first part is much the same. The person becomes depressed day and night. He sees the hopelessness of life and the horror of his own sins. But, by grace, he turns fully to Christ – instead of suicide. **In this way the depression leading to suicide or conversion is much the same in the beginning.**

Let this thought come to you when you are laughing with your friends – "Oh, but I'm not converted yet!" When you are at work, or at school, or at play, may you think, "Oh, but I'm not converted yet!" And every night, as you drift off to sleep, may you think, "Oh, but I'm not converted yet!" May this thought also come into your mind when you first wake up in the morning. Every day and every night – wherever you are and whatever you are doing – keep thinking, "I am not yet converted." Everything you look at or think about should remind you that you are unconverted – until you are out of this dreadful condition.

8. **Think farther, that the unconverted person who neglects salvation will increase his misery and pain.** To be unconverted while living among lost people is no surprise, any more than to be in the dark at midnight. But to be unconverted while in a church where the gospel is preached leaves you with no excuse, and will make your misery even greater in Hell.

God has not left you in darkness. But you close your eyes, and turn away from the truth, and refuse to think seriously about these things.

You must understand that the preaching you hear will either convert you or condemn you. Your refusal to be

27

converted makes your rebellion even greater, and your sin even worse than the sin of those who do not attend a gospel-preaching church.

Remember this, if you die unconverted, you will be condemned. *Those who have heard the most sermons will have the worst place in Hell – the greatest condemnation.*

9. *Remember that the farther you go in an unconverted state, the greater will be your punishment.* As long as you remain unconverted, you live in continual rebellion against God. You reject His mercy. You prefer the world of sin to Him.

Unconverted people think bad thoughts about real Christians. But they treat themselves even worse. They laugh at us, but they hurt and wound themselves. They tempt others to sin, but plunge into it themselves. They think lightly of the sermons they hear, and send themselves into the flames of Hell.

Also, think about the fact that while you remain unconverted, you grow more and more hardened in sin each day. God forsakes you more and more. The Spirit withdraws from you. Continuing in sin will make you worse and worse.

10. *As long as you remain unconverted, you rob yourself of happiness.* God offers you this happiness, and you could have it. But you keep yourself from having this happiness by rejecting conversion. You could have God instead of the world, Christ instead of sinful self, and the Holy Spirit instead of Satan who deceives you. You could have holiness instead of wickedness, justification instead of condemnation, blessings instead of a curse, peace of conscience instead of terror or false security. You don't really know what you lose every day by staying unconverted. You lose more than all the pleasures that sin can give you.

Ask those who have been converted if you don't believe me. Ask them if they would like to return to an unconverted state. If these people found that they were no better off than they were before, they would want to go back to an unconverted state. But true converts wouldn't do that for anything!

If you only knew how dangerous it is to go on like you are, you would leave your sinful life as quickly as a man would run out of a house on fire, or as a man would leave a boat sinking in the sea, knowing that if he did not hurry to get to shore, he would be drowned. And if you knew how wonderful it is to be converted, you would not wait even one day longer.

I have now showed you the dangers of remaining unconverted. If you dare to go on in unbelief, and carelessly reject what I said – if God leaves you to yourself, or if death comes to you while you are still lost – then you have no one to blame but yourself.

CHAPTER TWO

SELF-APPLICATION – "AM I CONVERTED?"

The purpose of this chapter is to get you to ask yourself, "Am I converted?" The Bible says:

> "Examine yourselves, whether ye be in the faith; prove
> your own selves" (II Corinthians 13:5).

The greatest proof of the existence of Heaven is the Bible – because it is the Word of God. I know that human beings have a tendency not to believe in things they can't see. But this weakness can be overcome by those who think.

What if you had never been to London, and yet you heard it described by someone else? Would you doubt that it existed because you hadn't seen it yourself? A person who is born blind has never seen the sun, and yet he doesn't doubt the existence of the sun when others tell him they have seen it. Shouldn't the Word of God be taken as seriously as the word of a man? You never saw God, and yet it is the worst error in the world to think there is no God (cf. Psalm 14:1; Psalm 53:1; Psalm 10:4). You can see the world that God made all around you, which could not have made itself. You know that there must have been a Creator from the evidence of creation.

Noah had never seen rain before the Flood (cf. Genesis 2:6). But when God told him that the Flood was coming, he worked many years to build an ark. The unbelieving world mocked him at the beginning, but when the Flood came they were convinced –when it was too late.

> "By faith Noah, being warned of God of things not seen
> as yet, moved with fear, prepared an ark to the saving
> of his house; by the which he condemned the world,
> and became heir of the righteousness which is by faith"
> (Hebrews 11:7).

If Satan can make you doubt the reality of Heaven and Hell, because you haven't seen them, he will be able to ruin you with the empty things of this world. But if you believe what the Bible says about eternal things, you will probably become a Christian very soon.

There is a Kingdom of Heaven. The Word of God says so. And Christ said that only those who are converted will enter it:

> "Verily I say unto you, Except ye be converted...ye shall not enter into the kingdom of heaven" (Matthew 18:3).

Reasons for Testing Whether You Are Converted or Not

I have showed you that there is a Kingdom of Heaven, and that only those who are converted can enter it. Now I ask you whether *you are converted or not.* You should ask yourself this question for several reasons.

1. The first reason is because of *the seriousness of it.* A wise person might take a risk on something small, but he wouldn't risk his life and everything he has if he could help it. Certainly no intelligent person would risk losing his soul.

   Eternal happiness or eternal misery is something you should think about very seriously. You should think about it soberly, and not treat it lightly. I often wonder how you can think about salvation so little, as if Heaven or Hell were unimportant. It seems to me that a person who believes that the dead go to Heaven or Hell would be eager to know where he is going when he dies, because once you are dead the question of where you go is settled forever.

   As long as you are in doubt about salvation, this thought should be in your mind all the time, "What will happen to me if I die without being converted? Where will I spend eternity?" You probably think that you are converted already. But what if you are deceived? I believe this thought should trouble you, "What if I'm wrong? What if I should perish in Hell?" What intelligent person would leave his everlasting salvation

31

or damnation in uncertainty, if he could possibly know the truth about his condition? Having comfort in your mind depends on being certain of your salvation, and your salvation depends on being very careful to make sure you are converted.

2. The second reason you should make very sure that you are saved is that *most people live and die without being converted.* You ought to take the words of Jesus Christ very seriously:

> "Strait (small) is the gate, and narrow is the way, which leadeth unto life, and *few there be that find it*" (Matthew 7:14).

I wish that all people were converted, but very few are. Look around you at the way people live. Listen to what they believe. You will see that this is true. Unless you have lost your mind, there is no excuse for standing around arguing about this instead of making sure of your *own* salvation. The reason that so few are converted is that they will not be saved on God's terms. And if you argue with God about this, instead of submitting to Him, you will be carried away to eternal ruin when you die. But those who care about their souls will be warned by the ruin of others, and be awakened to make sure of their own conversions.

3. Another reason you should make certain whether you are converted is that *failing to do this is one of the greatest reasons so few are converted.* Nothing is more certain to cause a person to turn around than realizing that he has lost his way. As long as you think you are travelling on the correct road you will never turn back to find the right one. That is the reason most people in the world never turn around and really get saved. They go on their way, and never once think seriously about asking a minister whether they are on the right path or not, or whether they will ever get to Heaven the way they are going. Surely if you will not even ask yourself whether you are saved, or will not take time to check

whether you are right or wrong, it is not likely that you will ever be converted. If you have never had the great work of conversion occur in your soul, you should not rest until it is done. If you thought very much about this, you could not lie down or rise up quietly. You could not eat, or sleep quietly. Tell me, *could* you be calm and quiet if you knew you were unconverted, and that if death should come to you, you would be damned in Hell? If you knew you were unconverted, how could you keep from crying out to Jesus, "Help me Lord, or I will spend eternity in damnation. Oh, forgive me, and change my heart and life, or I am lost forever!" If you knew that you were unconverted, wouldn't you cry out to Christ day and night until He changed your heart? You could not sit at home, but you would go to the minister and ask him for help and advice concerning your salvation. But when people think they are all right, they won't go to that much trouble.

I fear that many of you will remain unconverted because you believe the lie that you are already saved, when you are not. Believing this lie hinders my work, and ruins your soul. Therefore, for the Lord's sake, don't deny my request: take a little trouble to examine whether you are converted or not, for if anyone thinks he is something when he is nothing, he deceives himself.

4. Another reason you should not rest until you are sure you are converted is *the many benefits which the true knowledge of this would give you.* Oh, if you had the assurance of this, you could live quietly and have great comfort. You could lie down, and nothing would make you afraid. You could rejoice in God's mercy and know that He treats you like a father. You could hear and read the Bible with comfort. You could pray to God with comfort, and come with boldness to the throne of grace in prayer (cf. Hebrews 10:19; Ephesians 3:12). You could go to God in every time of sorrow, and pray to Him as your Father, in confidence that He will hear

33

you. You could gladly take communion with the members of your church. You could joyfully sing the hymns of worship and praise, and enjoy the fulness of salvation. And when you are dying, you could look forward to Heaven as your eternal home, and long to be with Christ (Philippians 1:23), and joyfully let go of your departing soul, as Jesus did when He said, "Father, into thy hands I commend my spirit" (Luke 23:46). Oh, what a wonderful life this is, when a person can look on every thing with comfort and Christian joy!

What would you give to be in such a condition? Wouldn't it be better to be converted than to have anything else in all the world? Wouldn't you rather have the hope of eternal life than anything else? Who cares what happens to you if you are sure of going to Heaven? Who cares what happens to this corruptible body if you are sure that all is well with your soul, and know that your body itself will rise again to glory? Oh, what a terrible thing for a soul to go out of the body, and not know where it is going! How awful it is to die under the curse of God, cursed by the Law, to the Last Judgment, to be condemned by the Judge. But how blessed to be converted, to die and be removed from this sinful world, to live with Christ, and to be "equal unto the angels" (Luke 20:36).

What do you say? Isn't there enough weight in these reasons to convince you to examine yourself, to see whether you are converted or not? Do you dare to say there isn't? Your own conscience will one day agree that I was not unreasonable to ask you to examine yourself.

Preliminary Tests of Conversion

But you may ask, "When I am examining my conscience, how can I know whether I am converted or not? By what tests can conversion be known?" Here are some brief answers to those questions. When you are examining yourself, you should ask,

1. *Whether you have had a change of mind in the following ways.* Are you convinced of the truth of the

Bible, God's Word, and about the things it says concerning the life to come? Do you know and believe how terrible a thing sin is? Are you convinced of your need for Christ, and what He has done for you, and what He offers you? Do you think more highly of God and salvation than anything else in the world? Do you think of everything else as worthless in comparison to being with Christ? Are you fully convinced of the riches of free grace in Christ, and are you convinced of the necessity of a holy life, no matter how much you neglected these things before?

2. *Do you look for happiness in Heaven, rather than looking for it in the things of this world?* Does God have the highest place in your heart, so that you do not prefer the world to Him? Have you decided that God should be served rather than the world? Have you tasted of the love which God has shown for you in the Blood of His Son? Have you come to Jesus Christ, as the only way to escape from the curse of the Law and the wrath of God? Have you given up all hopes of being saved by your own merits or righteousness? Have you taken Christ, the Son of God and His merits, as your only hope of salvation? Do you find that you hate the sins that you once loved, and enjoy the holy way of living, which you despised before? And are you convinced that you should live like this until you die?

3. *Is all of this true in your own life? Has there truly been a change in your way of living and a resolution never to return to your old ways?* Have you given up your ungodly friends? Especially, do you avoid those great sins by which you were carried away in the past? Are you willing to destroy what is left of your sins, whatever it costs you, so that there is no known sin that you wilfully live in, and no known duty that you wilfully neglect? Do you strongly desire to be what God wants you to be, and is it greatly troubling to you that you are no better than you are?

35

These are the main points of conversion, and this is the state of a converted soul. I have left out some particular points, to avoid being too long. When you examine your life to see if you are converted, ask yourself these questions and think deeply about the answers you give. All the difficulties you have will be connected with your heart. It is so dark and deceitful, that without special grace, you can easily be mistaken in your self-examination.

Again, I ask you to remember that you must be converted or condemned. Therefore, I ask you to be very serious about examining whether your conversion is real. I hope you are not willing to be deceived. I also hope you will not think salvation isn't worth so much effort. Tell me, therefore, will you do this much at Christ's command, or won't you? (cf. II Corinthians 13:5). Will you give some time to self-examination, until you know for sure whether your conversion is real or not?

I don't want you to spend another day in a lost condition, condemned and not knowing it. If you are converted, I want you to know it. If you are not, I want you to be aware of it. I want you to be sure whether or not you are really going to Heaven when you die, before you pass another week, or even before you go to bed tonight. And if you are not converted yet, I want you to know it, so that you will think seriously about conversion and not put off seeking Christ.

Don't think that I want to drive you to complete despair. If you find out that you are lost, you shouldn't say, "There's no hope." There is mercy waiting for you. Christ has prepared it for you, and He offers it to you, and He will give it to you if you are willing to receive it.

But you must allow yourself to be changed, and you must resolve not to go any farther in your old sinful way. It is conversion, and not despair, that God requires. It is only a foolish traveller who says, "I will not ask for directions, because if I find out that I went the wrong way, then I won't have any hope of getting home." A wise traveller will ask for the right directions, so he can know the right road, and get on it before it is late at night.

Further Tests of Conversion

It is my duty to convince unconverted people of their mistake, rather than comfort those who are already converted. Therefore I will give you these ***negative tests to show who is still unconverted:***

1. *Those who have never yet seen and felt that their sin is a great evil, deserving the wrath of God, are not converted.* Those who have never deeply felt their need to be pardoned from their sins by the Blood of Christ have never been converted. Those who have never been humbled because of their rebellion against God are still unconverted, and without conversion they cannot be saved (cf. Matthew 11:28; Luke 13:3,5; Psalm 51:17; Isaiah 57:15; Luke 14:11; Luke 18:14).

2. *Those who have never had the conceit of self-sufficiency beaten out are still unconverted.* Those who think *they* can do something, make some decision, commitment, or say a prayer, which brings about their salvation, are still unconverted. Those who do not admire God's glorious plan of redemption, which brings the news of salvation to ruined and distressed sinners, are not converted. Those whose hearts have never been warmed by a sense of Christ's love, but who hear the gospel as a mere story, which has nothing much to do with them, are unconverted. The person who has never been brought to Christ by God's drawing power for deliverance from sin and its penalty, is not converted (cf. Philippians 3:8-9; Ephesians 3:18-19; Luke 7:47-48; Romans 10:15; Acts 13:32).

3. *The person who does not have his heart and hopes in Heaven is not converted.* The person who does not look forward to Heaven, as the only place where he will have true happiness, is not converted. The person who does not make getting to Heaven the main purpose of his life, but whose goal is obtaining things in this world, is certainly unconverted, whatever he may pretend (cf. Philippians 3:20; Matthew 6:21; Romans 5:2; Titus 1:3; Hebrews 11; I Corinthians 15:19; Colossians 1:5,23).

4. *The person who is not weary and sick of all known sin, and does not hate sin, has never been converted.* The person who doesn't want to get rid of sin with all his heart, and is not willing to work hard to conquer sin,

has never been converted. He who thinks that it is all right to risk his soul by sinning, and who thinks that living a clean and holy life in the fellowship of the local church is too hard, is not yet converted, but must have a thorough change before he can be brought into conversion, and a state of life (cf. Luke 18:23-24; Romans 6:14,16,17,21; 7:13,22,24; Psalm 119:5).

5. *The person who does not eagerly and strongly engage in the duties of holiness to God, and righteousness and mercy toward man (such as membership and regular attendance in a local church every week, private and public prayer at prayer meetings, tithing, witnessing, clean living, etc.) has never been converted.* He who does not have the Spirit of Christ, nor the image of God upon himself, and does not express this in his worship and obedience, and is not merciful to others, nor humble in his own eyes, and does not enjoy doing good, *I say that person is not truly converted, whatever appearances of conversion he may have.* He must be converted or condemned (cf. Matthew 5:20; Hebrews 12:14; I Peter 1:15,16; 2:5; II Peter 3:11; Hebrews 3:1; Psalm 1:2).

6. *Those who have something in this world that they love so much that they will not give it up for Christ, but will risk their souls, and only do as much as they think they have to do, and are not ready to let everything go for Christ, are not converted.* They must be changed or condemned (cf. Matthew 16:24; 10:37-38; Luke 14:33; Philippians 3:19; Matthew 13:6,20,21).

My heart is full of pain over the thought that great multitudes of sinners are yet in a state of death, never having been converted. What do you think when you read the Scriptures I have referred to? You must realize that they speak to you as well as others. What, then, do you think of yourself? Are you converted?

Dr. Hymers' note: Since the time of Charles G. Finney (1792-1875), evangelicals have gradually given up the idea of conversion held by all Baptists and Protestants for over four hundred years, and expressed so well by Baxter in this chapter. Today, evangelicals in general have adopted the false view that some converts are changed while others remain unchanged. This unscriptural idea of conversion, which first came as a result of the ministry of Finney, must be rejected, and the old Biblical view of Baptists and Protestants, as presented by Baxter, must be returned to, or millions of unconverted souls in our churches will go to eternal punishment in Hell.

It is important that you think about the things that deceive lost people into thinking they are saved. Here are three main things which trick people into thinking they are saved when they aren't:

1. They do not know what true conversion is, but think that it is something which it isn't.

2. They do not know themselves deeply and honestly, and so they think they possess what they do not.

3. They have already decided what they believe about conversion, therefore they think they are saved already, and will, for that reason, not examine themselves to see whether they are truly converted or not.

In the previous pages I have showed that true conversion is rare, and that most of the world is unconverted, and will go to Hell. In my mind, I see thousands of faces standing before the Judgment seat of God, who will say,

> "Depart from me, ye cursed, into everlasting fire"
> (Matthew 25:41).

Am I wrong to tell you that you are not converted when I know that you face this punishment? Should I hold back, and try not to offend you, and let you go on, until you fall into the flames of perdition?

If you don't feel any danger, it doesn't mean that you are safe. It only means that you are spiritually asleep, and that you must be awakened. If you won't believe what I have taught you from the Scriptures, you wouldn't be persuaded even though someone rose from the dead (ref. Luke 16:31).

A true minister is like a physician who sees a foolish man eating arsenic, and tells him it is a deadly poison. "You must not eat it or it will kill you," he says. But because the poison tastes good, the fool tells the physician that he is wrong, and goes on eating the sweet poison until he feels it burning in his stomach, and it is too late to save him. Think of the pain you will feel in Hell, when you remember how you rejected this book. Who is it that has done you wrong? Is it me, who told you of your danger, or is it yourself, who rejected what I said, and refused the cure?

CHAPTER THREE

THE NECESSITY OF CONVERSION

> "If any man be in Christ, he is a new
> creature: old things are passed away;
> behold, all things are become new"
> (II Corinthians 5:17).

By now you can see that conversion is a great change which is made in the soul, and in the life, by the renewing grace of Christ. If you haven't been changed by conversion, you should remember what He said:

> "Except ye be converted, and become as little children,
> ye shall not enter into the kingdom of heaven"
> (Matthew 18:3).

Your words and your life show that you are not yet converted. What is it that lets you remain in peace? How can anyone read such a verse as this without being awakened from false security? Yet by experience I know that you can read Matthew 18:3, knowing that you aren't converted, and still be as careless as if it didn't matter that you are eternally lost. Why does this happen? Undoubtedly it is because you do not completely believe the truth of what I have said. Therefore,

I. I will show from the Word of God the absolute necessity of conversion.

What further proof do you need that conversion is necessary than the words of this verse?

> "Except ye be converted...ye shall not enter into the
> kingdom of heaven" (Matthew 18:3).

Christ told Nicodemus that he couldn't enter the kingdom of heaven unless he was regenerated (i.e. born again). This means that as a child receives new life, is a new creature, and enters newly into the world, so everyone who wishes to be saved must receive a new spiritual life, and enter into the world of grace, and begin life anew.

> "If any man be in Christ, he is a new creature: old things
> are passed away; behold, all things are become new"
> (II Corinthians 5:17).

In this verse we see both the necessity and nature of the change that occurs in conversion. It is not just a few persons who need it, but everyone, "*If any man...*" And he that is not in Christ is not a Christian, "If any man be in Christ..." If he is not a Christian, he cannot be saved. *Every true Christian, then, is a new creature in character and in life:* "Old things are passed away; behold, all things are become new." What are "old things"? They are your old sins and your sinful life-style in the past. A truly converted person will not have the same motives he had before.

You will have new hope and happiness, new love, new desires, new sorrow, new delight, new resolution, and a new way of living and talking. Everything will become new to you when you are converted. You will have a new covenant with Christ, a new master, a new head and Lord, and you will be a member of a new society (the local church), and you will enter into a new kingdom and family. You will have a new work to do, a new group of friends in the church, new thoughts in your heart, and a new way of speaking.

Conversion is putting off the old man and putting on the new man:

> "...seeing that ye have put off the old man with his
> deeds; and have put on the new man, which is renewed
> in knowledge after the image of him that created him"
> (Colossians 3:9-10).

Knowing this, that the converted person's "old man" is crucified with Christ, that from now on he should not serve sin – for he that is dead is freed from sin (cf. Romans 6:4-7). Thus, those who are converted serve God in newness of spirit (Romans 7:6). But in case there is any doubt in your mind, I will give you some points to show the necessity of conversion.

42

1. *Conversion is the very thing that Christ came into the world to give, to bring wicked sinners to God.* Do you think that Christ came to do something that was not necessary? Just as His suffering was necessary to pay for our sins, so His doctrine and Spirit are necessary for our conversion. We can no more be saved without the one than without the other. Would God have sent His Son to earth on purpose to call home wandering sinners if they could be saved without conversion? The Lord Jesus is the great physician of souls. He did not come to heal small diseases which might have been healed without Him. He came to cure the destructive plague of sin, which no one else could cure but Him. It was never in the mind of Christ to come down from Heaven to suffer for our sins, that we might continue to live in them without a change. He never expected to bring people to Heaven in their sins, but to destroy their sins. He never meant to bring you and your disease together into Heaven, but to heal your disease, which otherwise would have ruined you. What greater blasphemy against Christ can there be than to imagine that He befriends sin, which He hates so much? What greater blasphemy can there be than to imagine that Christ stands with Satan and strengthens the Devil's kingdom – when it was truly His mission to destroy it?

Thus, Christ came to convert people, and not to pardon them without conversion. "The Son of man is come to seek and to save that which was lost" (Luke 19:10). "Who gave himself for us," not to pardon and save us without converting us, but "that he might redeem us from all iniquity, and purify unto himself a peculiar people, zealous of good works" (Titus 2:14). From these verses you can see the absolute necessity of conversion if you hope to be saved.

2. *Conversion is the main thing in the whole Bible, to convert people from sin to God, and to build them up once they are converted.* And do you think that God

would have made conversion the main topic of the Bible if it were not necessary to be converted? If a person could be saved without conversion, why would God have inspired prophets and apostles to deliver His Word to convert people and build up the converted? Would God do all the things recorded in the Bible for something that is not needed? This is the very purpose of God's Word: "The law of the Lord (the Bible) is perfect, converting the soul" (Psalm 19:7). What else does the Bible tell lost sinners to do, but to repent and turn to Jesus Christ? Hundreds of verses in the Bible show that the main purpose of the Scriptures is to turn sinners to Christ (cf. Ezekiel 33:11; Isaiah 31:6; 59:20-21; Jeremiah 3:7; Proverbs 1:23; Joel 2:12-13; Jonah 3:8; Acts 3:19; etc.).

3. *Conversion is the business to which ministers of the gospel are called, to convert people to Christ.* Why would God call men to preach conversion if it were not necessary? John the Baptist began preaching repentance. Christ followed him, preaching the same thing (Luke 13:3-5). The apostles followed Him, preaching the same repentance, without which there is no salvation (Acts 2:38; 8:22). They tell us that God "commandeth all men every where to repent" (Acts 17:30). Paul's work was to show people that they "should repent and turn to God, and do works meet for repentance' (Acts 26:20). And "to open their eyes, and to turn them from darkness to light, and from the power of Satan unto God, that they may receive forgiveness of sins..." (Acts 26:18). The substance of Paul's preaching was, "Repentance toward God, and faith toward our Lord Jesus Christ" (Acts 20:21). Ministers are to be found "in meekness instructing those that oppose themselves; if God peradventure will give them repentance to the acknowledging of the truth; And that they may recover themselves out of the snare of the devil, who are taken captive by him at his will" (II Timothy 2:25-26). So, the main business of preachers is to convert people to Christ.

4. *The conversion of others is the work and duty of every Christian.* Would God tell us this if there were any other way of salvation? "They that be wise shall shine as the brightness of the firmament; and they that turn many to righteousness, as the stars for ever and ever" (Daniel 12:3). "If any of you do err from the truth, and one convert him; let him know that he which converteth the sinner from the error of his way shall save a soul from death, and shall hide a multitude of sins" (James 5:19-20).

Put all this together, and decide whether it would be likely that God would have sent His churches to work for the conversion of sinners, if there had been any other way to save them. *Would Christ Himself have come to convert people if they didn't need it?* Would the Bible have been given for this reason – to convert people? Would the prophets, and apostles, and ministers of the gospel be sent with this message of conversion? Would it be the duty of every Christian to work for conversion, if people could be saved without it?

Therefore, let it be a firm belief in your heart that you cannot be saved without being converted.

II. **I will give several reasons why a person cannot enter the kingdom of heaven without being converted.**

1. *If we had nothing but the Bible, as the only reason, it would be enough.* Heaven belongs to God, and He can give it to whoever He will. And He has told us in His Word that He will give it to no one but him who is converted.

   "Except ye be converted...ye shall not enter into the kingdom of heaven" (Matthew 18:3).

Do you object to this doctrine, that none will be saved but the converted? Then you are finding fault with God. Do you think you are wiser than Him? Do you

45

think He doesn't know what He's doing? Will you accuse Him of injustice – a guilty sinner like you, who has done so much wrong to the Lord, and who has refused His grace? You should not dare to open your mouth against God, and tell Him, after all this, that if He condemns you He is unmerciful!

I will tell you my religion. I believe all that God says in the Bible is true, whether I completely understand it or not. I have looked to see if there is any better or surer foundation for real Christianity, and I have found none. When God tells me in His Word that no man will be saved except he is converted, I take Him at His Word. I will set the Word of God against all the reasoning in the world. If you think it's difficult to believe that so few are saved, and that you cannot believe God will deal so harshly, against all your arguments I will simply quote the Word of God. God will do what He says in the Bible.

2. *The second reason that no one can enter the kingdom of Heaven without being converted is from the nature of God's government.* Do you want God to reward people for serving Satan? Do you want God to say, at the Last Judgment, "Come, sinner. You have lived for the Devil all your life, and have thought only about the pleasures of this world. You have despised me and my church. But come in – enter into the glory of Heaven"? Do you think God should say that? Sinner, if self-love didn't blind you, you would see that a decision like that would be unfit for a righteous God. Do you think He will reward the Devil's servants? "Shall not the Judge of all the earth do right?" (Genesis 18:25). And what is right, but to give every person what he deserves?

3. *But further, consider this. The holy nature of God will not permit an unholy soul to enter into His presence.* "There shall in no wise enter into it [Heaven] any thing that defileth, neither whatsoever worketh abomination" (Revelation 21:27). "Thou art of purer

eyes than to behold evil, and canst not look on iniquity" (Habakkuk 1:13). "The righteous Lord loveth righteousness; but the wicked and him that loveth violence his soul hateth" (Psalm 5:4,5; 11:5,7). "Therefore the ungodly shall not stand in the judgment, nor sinners in the congregation of the righteous" (Psalm 1:5). "The wicked shall be turned into hell, and all the nations that forget God" (Psalm 9:8,16,17). What more reasons would you have? There is opposition between the nature of God and the unconverted. "What fellowship hath righteousness with unrighteousness? and what communion hath light with darkness?" (II Corinthians 6:14).

Either you must become holy like God or God must become unholy like you – or you will not be able to live together in Heaven. God cannot become unholy, because it is against His very nature. You must become holy in His sight, through the imputed righteousness of Christ, which you receive at conversion. For this reason, only converted people can live with God in Heaven. If you turn to Christ you will be welcome in Heaven. But never expect that God will become sinful like you.

4. *Here is another reason unconverted people cannot go to Heaven. God offered them salvation in this life and they refused it.* God made it simple for them to be saved, but they refused it. They could have had Christ and forgiveness, and holiness and happiness, if they wanted it, but they rejected it all. God set life and death before them and asked them to choose life that they should live (Deuteronomy 30:19). But they deliberately chose death. God called His preachers to deal with them in season, and out of season (II Timothy 4:2), and to "reprove, rebuke, exhort with all longsuffering and doctrine." He even told His ministers to "compel them to come in" (Matthew 22:9; Luke 14:23). And yet they would not come. Some made one excuse for not being converted. Some made another excuse. Some did not

47

take our message seriously. Others attacked and opposed it.

It grieves me to say that I must witness against thousands of people like this. Sinner, I tell you this day, that God and angels and men will know that if you are thrust into Hell it will be the result of your rejection of salvation in Christ. You will not go to Hell because God is cruel to you, but because you were cruel to yourself.

5. *If all these reasons for God not permitting unconverted people into the kingdom of Heaven don't satisfy you, I will give one more – it is an impossible thing.* It is a contradiction. Sin is the soul's sickness and death, and conversion and holiness are its life. Only a fool would try to make a dead body come to life. Yet it is as great an impossibility for a man to be saved without being converted. What must we be saved from, if it isn't sin and Hell? And there is no salvation from Hell without salvation from sin. "He shall save his people from their sins" (Matthew 1:21).

CHAPTER FOUR

THE NATURE OF CONVERSION –
A CHANGE OF THE MIND

"Verily I say unto you, Except ye be
converted, and become as little children,
ye shall not enter into the kingdom of
heaven" (Matthew 18:3).

I don't need to beg you to love yourself, and seek happiness.
You will do those things without me telling you, because they are in
your own interest. Only a fool doesn't love himself and want to be
happy. My purpose is to tell you where happiness comes from and
where it does not – and to advise you to go in the direction that will
bring you the greatest joy.

My motive is to please God and save souls. I don't think it's
right to enter the pulpit for any other purpose. A man who preaches
with any other intent is seeking something for himself, and not for
Christ. No wonder such "preachers" use smooth words and charming
phrases. They are trying to please the people rather than God.

I know how hard it is to get people to listen to the truth about
conversion. I know how cold people are even when they owe their
very souls to a faithful preacher. But I remember that I must speak in
the name of Christ. I also remember that I must speak to people who
will either be everlastingly happy or everlastingly miserable.

I know how little time you have to change your eternal destiny. I
know also that the Bible tells us very few people will be saved, that
many "are called, but few are chosen" (Matthew 20:16; Matthew
22:14). Most people are lost forever because they will not think about
Christ, or accept the mercy He offers them.

That's why I speak to you on only one subject – the one upon
which your life or death depends. If I wanted you to think of me as a
great scholar, or to get you to applaud what I say, I would speak on a
more pleasing subject, and I would tell you some exciting stories and
funny jokes. But I know that this would please the Devil, rather than

God, so I will not speak that way at all. I pray for God to use what I say to convert your soul. That's what I want to happen.

> "Verily I say unto you, Except ye be converted, and become as little children, ye shall not enter into the kingdom of heaven" (Matthew 18:3).

This verse speaks of coming into a state of salvation, because conversion is the entrance into the preparatory kingdom.

I. The Doctrine of Conversion

We can learn several doctrines from this text in Matthew 18:3.

1. Unless people are converted, they cannot enter into the kingdom of heaven.

2. All people are by nature in the kingdom of Satan. When they are converted they are transferred into the kingdom of heaven. A person is moved from the kingdom of Satan to the kingdom of heaven by experiencing conversion.

3. The words conversion, repentance, regeneration, and sanctification are used in the Bible to explain the same work of God in the human soul. But each word shows something slightly different about this one work.

4. *"Conversion"* (Greek epistrephō) means "to turn around and towards." There are two sides of conversion. One is turning *from* a state of sin and misery (it can also refer to turning from individual sins), and the other is turning *to* Jesus Christ. We turn around from sin and come to Christ in true conversion.

5. *"Repentance"* (Greek metanoia) describes our change of thinking – from loving sin to loving Christ, and hating sin. The word "repentance" means that we have a new mind, a new way of looking at Christ, and at sin. In repentance, we come to hate sin and love Christ, hate the world and love the local church.

"Repentance" speaks of two things: (1) Deep *sorrow* that we have sinned; (2) A change of mind *from* that sin *to* Jesus Christ. The first is only a part of the second. The changed mind is sorrowful over past sins, although sorrow is not all there is to such a change. Yet whenever real repentance occurs, part of the change of mind does include deep sorrow for sins.

6. *"Regeneration"* (Greek palingenesia) also means the same thing as "conversion." But there is this small difference. The term "regeneration" means "new birth." So great is the change, that a person is a new man. Although the term "regeneration" is more comprehensive than "conversion," the two words mean essentially the same thing.

7. *"Sanctification"* (Greek hagiasmos) also means the same thing as "conversion," but with this small difference: the word focuses on our deep love for God, and the holiness of life which comes from such love. The Greek word in the New Testament refers to the separation of the convert from sin, and his separation to God.

Now I must show you what it means to be "converted and become as little children." This can't be done very well unless I first give you a description of the state of an unconverted person.

Man sinned, broke the law of God, and made himself a ruined slave of Satan and a child of death. Therefore, the very nature of an unconverted person is corrupted and depraved. We are unclean in our very natures. Conversion deals with the question, "Who can bring a clean thing out of an unclean?" (Job 14:4). How could Adam pass on to the human race a good nature when he had lost this himself? We are all born with corrupted characters which we inherited from Adam. Our natures are against God and heavenly things, and are interested only in this world and earthly things. Pride, covetousness, unbelief, error, hypocrisy, ungodliness, fighting, and all wickedness have their roots inside of us.

If temptation comes you will commit sin, because you have a depraved nature. You cannot stop living in sin before God gives you conversion.

Since your very nature is sinful, it will only get worse the longer you sin, and the longer you put off being converted.

Since your nature is dead, something outside of yourself must convert you, for a corrupted tree cannot bring forth good fruit. The main cause of conversion is the Holy Spirit. The Holy Spirit uses sermons on Jesus Christ to convert people. The Holy Spirit causes a person to believe in Jesus. The Holy Spirit turns a person away from trust in himself to trust in Jesus Christ instead. The Holy Spirit makes conversion occur within the sinner, to bring about this inward change.

The parts of conversion are these:

1. It is a change of mind;
2. It is a change of heart;
3. It is a change of life.

II. Conversion Changes the Mind

Every unconverted person is *ignorant* of the saving truths of the gospel of Christ, either because he has not heard of it, or because he has not understood it.

Most people in the world do not know that man's nature is totally corrupted. They do not know how God hates sin, and how sin deserves God's everlasting wrath. They do not know how Jesus Christ satisfies God's justice and redeems us from misery. They do not know that Jesus offers them pardon through His death on the Cross, and on what terms that pardon is offered to them, or how those who believe in Christ will enter everlasting glory, and those who do not believe in Him will be in everlasting misery. Many are completely ignorant of these fundamental principles of the Christian religion. Most of those who do know them, know them only in a shallow and ineffective way.

1. *The first thing that the Spirit of God does in conversion is to open your eyes to understand these truths; so that those of you who used to hear sermons as an unreal thing, now hear them like someone who is brought out of a dark dungeon into the open light.*

52

You will be like someone who was blind but has recovered his eyesight, who is happy to see the light and is surprised at how ignorant and blind he was before.

I will prove this to you by the Scriptures:

> "The natural [unconverted] man receiveth not the things of the Spirit of God; for they are foolishness unto him: neither can he know them, because they are spiritually discerned"
> (I Corinthians 2:14).

> "If our gospel be hid, it is hid to them that are lost: In whom the god of this world [Satan] hath blinded the minds of them which believe not, lest the light of the glorious gospel of Christ, who is the image of God, should shine unto them"
> (II Corinthians 4:3-4).

Then the Bible tells us of the opening of spiritual eyes, which happens in conversion:

> "I send thee to open their eyes, and to turn them from darkness to light, and from the power of Satan unto God"
> (Acts 26:17-18).

You are ignorant of the saving truths in the Bible until God Himself awakens you to their reality.

2. *In conversion your mind is also changed from thoughtlessness to serious attention.* The main reason we cannot get people to hate this world of sin and seek to find Christ is that we cannot get them to *think seriously.* Instead of thinking deeply about the sermon, lost people go home from church to talk about other subjects, and think about other things. They are not helped by the sermon because they don't *think* about it. *We can't get them to go alone for an hour and actually recall seriously what they heard.*

53

But when the Spirit of God comes to convert you, He causes you to *think* about the sermon. He wakes up your sleeping soul and shows you that the sermon is for *you*. God sets the truth of the sermon before your eyes and makes you contemplate *seriously* what you heard. God Himself focuses your thoughts on the sermon you heard, which before you would have forgotten right away. You might have heard a hundred sermons on sin and Christ, and the need to be converted, you may have heard about judgment and Heaven and Hell many times, but you never seriously thought about these things until now. But at this time God brings the sermon sharply and clearly into your mind.

This is a great part of the converting work of God's Spirit, to make a person actually *think* about the sermons he hears.

3. *The third change in the mind at conversion is from unbelief to true faith.* A word or two in the sermon about Heaven or Hell, if it were really believed by you, would make you search for Christ with all your heart. But unconverted sinners only "half believe" the Bible. They really don't fully believe what the Bible teaches.

But when the Spirit of God begins to work in you, then you will see that everything in the Bible is *really true*. You will begin to see that Christ and everlasting torment in Hell are not dreams, but *are actual facts*. Whatever you think about this now, all people on earth will soon find themselves in Heaven or Hell.

If you tell someone that a robber is following him, and he doesn't run away fast, you can be sure he didn't *really* believe you. But if you see that person run for his life, it is proof that he believes what you said. When a person is truly converted, you can easily see by the way he acts whether he believes what the Bible says. Because Noah truly believed what he heard, he was moved with fear and prepared for judgment (cf. Hebrews 11:7). If you saw Noah at work on the ark you would know that he *really believed* what he heard, otherwise he would not have worked so hard to escape from the danger.

4. *The fourth change that comes with conversion is a turning away from errors.* Before they are converted, lost people think that there is no Heaven or Hell. Or they think that God will save them the way they are.

But when God converts you, your opinions on these subjects will be changed. You once thought it was O.K. to miss church for any reason. You once thought it was all right to sin in one way or another. But when you are converted, you will turn away from these errors and sins. You will then think, "What a fool I was to sleep away the short time of my life instead of searching for salvation in Christ! What a fool I was to forget how close God's judgment is!"

When you are awakened by God, you will say, "I must hurry to make sure I am ready for Heaven! I must do all I can to make sure that I don't go into the flames of everlasting torment!"

My unsaved friend, your mind will be changed, you will think differently from the way you do now, when you are converted. You will have a new way of thinking about sin and church, the wicked and the godly.

You may say that you will never change your mind, but God Himself can make you think differently from the way you think now. God's light will not be overcome by your darkness, if He means for light to shine into your soul.

Jesus said:

> "Verily I say unto you, Except ye be converted, and become as little children, ye shall not enter into the kingdom of heaven" (Matthew 18:3).

CHAPTER FIVE

THE NATURE OF CONVERSION –
A CHANGE OF THE HEART

> "Love not the world, neither the things
> that are in the world. If any man love the
> world, the love of the Father is not in
> him" (I John 2:15).

The first part of the work of conversion is on the mind. The second part is on the heart. When I speak of the "heart" I am referring to your will, that part of you which makes choices. In conversion, it is necessary for the mind to be changed to prepare for the will to be changed. When you think differently, then you will act differently.

God brings the will to love what it once disliked, and to dislike what it loved before.

1. *The first change that God makes on the heart during conversion is in the desires. He causes you to love what you once thought was bitter.* Before conversion every craving you have is for earthly things and you have no appetite for the things of God. In fact, your heart is opposed to the things of God. You love to possess, or think about possessing, earthly things. You have no pleasure in God. You do not want to hear about, or think about, the life to come in Heaven. Before you are converted you do not enjoy God or holy things. You do not like to think of them, or to speak about them, or even hear about them very much. You wonder why other people enjoy hearing about holy subjects. You yourself hardly ever think about the things of God.

You may go to church once in a while and say a quick prayer, but you are glad when it's over. That is why the

Bible calls you an enemy of God – because your heart is against Him, even though you say you love Him (Isaiah 29:13).

> "This people draweth nigh unto me with their mouth, and honoureth me with their lips; but their heart is far from me" (Matthew 15:8).

I know it is very common for people to say that God has more of their hearts than He really does. They say they love Him when they really don't. Sin has so blinded them that they really don't know themselves.

If you could see yourself as you really are, you would realize that you have actually rejected God, and shut Him out of your life. Many sinners would rather lie to themselves rather than admit that they have no love for God. As the Psalmist said, "God is not in all his thoughts" (Psalm 10:4). "The Lord knoweth the thoughts of man, that they are vanity" (Psalm 94:11).

The first change that God makes on your heart is to turn it to Himself, and give your heart a new desire for Him and His ways. The Holy Spirit opens your eyes to see God's excellency, and the value of the glorious things He has promised in Heaven. It is a humanly impossible thing to make people to think seriously about Heaven, but God can do it, and God does do it when conversion takes place. Then you will truly say, "Whom have I in heaven but thee? and there is none upon earth that I desire beside thee" (Psalm 73:25).

You hardly ever thought of God before. Now that God is awakening you, you are concerned about whether He is reconciled to you or not, and what He thinks about your way of living. This is true of the converted soul. Other people *only talk about God* – but converted people *give Him their hearts.*

I am trying to make this as plain as I can to you, because *I want you to ask yourself whether you have been converted or not. Has this change occurred in you?* You know that there is something that is most important in your life. It is the thing you talk about most and think about most. If you had no real interest in it, you would not think about it or talk about it all the time.

Here is the real difference between the heart of a converted person and the unconverted heart. Before a person is converted his mind hardly ever thinks about God, but after conversion, nothing is more interesting than Him! The Bible describes these two states:

> "For they that are after the flesh do mind the things of the flesh; but they that are after the Spirit the things of the Spirit. For to be carnally minded is death; but to be spiritually minded is life and peace. Because the carnal mind is enmity against God: for it is not subject to the law of God, neither indeed can be. So then they that are in the flesh cannot please God. But ye are not in the flesh, but in the Spirit, if so be that the Spirit of God dwell in you. Now if any man have not the Spirit of Christ, he is none of his"
> (Romans 8:5-9).

Here you see, in the very words of the Bible, a plain description of these two different conditions – converted and unconverted. Until you are converted, your mind is concentrated on having pleasures in this world. Your mind is focused on your happiness in this life, not on the world to come. No matter what you say about loving God, He knows that you don't really love Him at all. But when conversion comes, it removes the old way of thinking and gives a new thought-pattern. Now the person who was carnally minded becomes spiritually minded.

Look into your own heart, and ask yourself what you would like to have if you could have anything in the world – what most pleases you – what you would desire if you could have your choice of anything you wanted.

By looking closely at this you can tell whether you are converted or not. You may think that you can have a worldly mind and still be a child of God. But don't deceive yourself. It cannot be. If you ever hope to escape the torments you deserve, and see God's face in Heaven, your heart must be turned another way! Your shameful delights must become bad tasting to you. You must be ashamed of what you now love.

Many weaknesses may exist in a converted person, but a carnal or worldly mind in a dominant sense cannot. "Love not the world, neither the things that are in the world. If any man love the world, the love of the Father is not in him" (I John 2:15).

Only a foolish man would say that God is not better than this world. But the question is this: which of these does he love more? Never tell me that your thoughts about God are sincere unless you think about Him with affection when you are alone.

When converting grace comes it does this work – it causes the heart to sincerely love God. When the best Christians have reached the highest knowledge of God and His love, they are still looking for more. And they see how little they have known. The converted soul knows the emptiness and worthlessness of this world when he is first humbled and made to see his sins, when he is made to see that he has broken God's law, and when he is in terror of God's anger. How can anything in the world bring him relief, or peace, or pleasure? If you are ever converted, God will show you another kind of pleasure. He will give your diseased soul a thirst for Jesus, the living water (John 4:14). "The love of God is shed abroad in our hearts by the Holy Ghost" (Romans 5:5).

2. *The second part of the change of the heart in conversion is in its purpose – what it wants to do.* Conversion causes a person to wish for what is right.

The converted person's desire is to seek the will of God and to do the right thing.

Before conversion, all people are inwardly and secretly enemies of God. Their hearts are against Him. It is not God whom they really search for, no matter what they may say. It is something in the world that they seek, and not God. Therefore they are said to "have their portion in this life" (Psalm 17:14).

You are therefore called "the men of the world." You build up some treasure on earth (Matthew 6:19). You think that there is nothing greater that you can do. You do not know the joy of God's presence. You seek only what you can eat or drink, or what you can wear, for this is the way of unconverted people on earth (Luke 12:29,30). You think very little of Christ and His kingdom, in comparison with the things you are interested in on earth. You do things for yourself, but you are not rich toward God (Matthew 22:5; Luke 12:21). *You do not want to give up anything for Christ.* Your "end is destruction, whose god is their belly, and whose glory is in their shame, who mind earthly things" (Philippians 3:19). You work only for good things in this life. You think that true Christians are foolish to give up pleasures to pray, and listen to sermons, and be in church. *Therefore when real Christians are comforted in Heaven, you will be tormented in Hell* (Luke 16:25). The Scriptures describe what unconverted men want and what their hearts desire. For where your treasure is, there will your heart be (Matthew 6:21).

But when converting grace comes, the very purposes of a man (*the things he wants to do*) are **changed!** He now **wants** to think about God and Heaven! He has figured out what the world is worth, what it can give him, and how long it will last him, or what it will do for him when he needs help. *He has decided that the world can never make him happy.* If you ever get converted you will experience all this yourself.

Converting grace makes a person think about whether anything in the entire world could truly satisfy him. When you begin to be awakened, in the beginning of conversion, you will realize that nothing in this world can truly fulfill your desires and dreams. God will now open your mind so that the false appearances of earthly things cannot deceive you as they used to. Now that God is awakening you, you think about how earthly pleasures and worldly friends lead only to the grave and Hell, and leave you when you are in the depths of distress.

Before you were like the Prodigal Son, who thought that it was difficult to live in his father's house. Away among his friends and pleasures he wanted to go. But when he was awakened, he *wanted to go home again!* He was dying with hunger for the things of God!

In this way God takes your soul, during conversion, away from its former purposes and desires, and makes you say, *"Lord, these things will not satisfy me. Please don't let me be content with things like this."* When your soul is loosened from its former delights, and sees that something else is needed for you to be truly happy, the Holy Spirit shows you that *Jesus Christ alone can satisfy.*

The very best of worldly things will no longer please you, because you will now "desire a better country, that is, an heavenly: wherefore God is not ashamed to be called their God; for he hath prepared for them a city" (Hebrews 11:16).

3. *The third part of the work of conversion in the heart is a new willingness to seek Christ the way God tells you in the Bible*. Salvation cannot be found any way you want. You must be saved God's way – or remain lost.

Two things are absolutely necessary in salvation:

a. You must believe the truths about Christ given in the Bible.

b. You must do *more* than that, however. You must believe in Jesus Christ *Himself* – up in Heaven. You must actually come to *Him.*

The truth is, your unconverted heart is against both of these things. You do not deeply believe in the substitutionary death, physical resurrection and bodily ascension of Christ. Your belief in these things is very shallow. Also, you do not seek Christ in Heaven – because you have not been humbled, and do not feel the need of Christ. "They that are whole have no need of a physician, but they that are sick" (Mark 2:17).

You have learned to say nice things about Christ, and you are even willing to be forgiven by Him, but you have never taken ahold of Him, like a drowning man would grab a piece of floating wood to save him from being sucked under the water.

But when converting grace comes, you will think very highly of Christ, and seek with all your might to know Him. Then you will say, *"I am tormented by my own conscience, and nothing but Thy blood can make my conscience stop accusing me. I am condemned by the law, which I have broken. I don't know what to do if Thy blood does not pardon me. I have thousands of sins against me. I cannot meet the demands of God's justice. I must have Thy sacrifice on the Cross as my substitute, for the payment of my sins. Hell is now ready to swallow me eternally if Thou dost not convert me. Save me, save me, Lord Jesus, or I will perish! A just and angry God will be an eternal consuming fire to me if His anger is not put out by Thy blood, O Christ!"*

Here are four things that happen when converting grace comes to you:

a. ***Self-condemnation for sin.*** Unconverted people feel no burden of conscience which drives them to Christ for forgiveness. Their consciences are dead. They are quick to point out other people's faults, but they are just as quick to excuse their own sins.

But when converting grace comes, your whole attitude will change. You will then talk very much against ***yourself.*** You will then speak a great deal about your own sins. You will condemn yourself!

b. ***Earnest prayer to God.*** Unconverted people don't know anything about true prayer. They either don't pray at all or else they pray mechanically, with no life in it. But when converting grace comes, you will cry out to God. Reality in prayer is one of the signs that converting grace has come.

c. ***Great interest in the Word of God.*** In your unconverted state, you have little interest in the Bible or the preaching of God's Word. You let your mind wander while reading the Bible, or while sitting in church as the sermon is preached. But when converting grace comes you will have great interest in reading the Bible and hearing the preaching of God's Word.

d. ***Fellowship with Christians.*** Unconverted people are very quick to judge real Christians, and often get angry with them instead of forgiving them. The truth is that they don't really like true Christians. The more holy the Christian is, the less an unconverted person will like him.

Unconverted people will look for faults in others as an excuse to leave the church, or commit other sins. *They are continually judging Christians so they can excuse themselves.*

It is natural for a wicked person to hate a true Christian (Genesis 3:15; I John 3:12; Hebrews 11:4). Christ told His disciples that the world would hate them because He had chosen them out of the world; but if they were part of the world, the world would love them (John 15:19). This explains why the unconverted world hates Christ and His true followers.

But when the soul is really converted there will be a strong love for real Christians and a deep love for the local church. A person who is truly converted will not leave his local church (I John 2:19), but he will stay because he truly loves the members (John 13:34-35; John 15:12-13). People who change membership often, because they find faults in the members or leaders, are *nearly always* unconverted people. There are very few exceptions. *When you are converted you will love your neighbor as yourself, in the local church.* This is all very practical in the life of a real convert.

4. *The fourth part of the work of conversion in the will is the settling of the heart – a great settled seriousness about being converted.*

This is not separate from what has been said. It is a summing up of all I have written so far.

Many people have some conviction or interest in being saved, but after a while this goes away, and they go back like they were without being converted. They remain half-converted, but they are still lost.

Sometimes God turns the heart quickly, and a person is suddenly converted. But most people linger a long time under conviction and partial awakening – before they are converted. They know that they are lost, but they stay in a dull, weak-minded condition, half-resolved, half in and half out of salvation.

But true conversion turns the mind over wholly to God, and shows you that there is no cure for sin but Jesus Christ. You will then know that there is no other pardon for sin but His blood. You will then realize that you must throw yourself on Jesus to be saved. You will then be determined to trust nothing else but Christ, Himself.

True conversion will make you say, "I am through with the world and a wasted life. Take the world, but give me Jesus!"

Many people have been lost forever who started out to find Christ. The main part of the work of saving grace lies in bringing about this resolution – "I will not stop seeking Christ until I find Him." *If you are ever converted, you will be determined to find Christ at any cost.*

65

CHAPTER SIX

THE NATURE OF CONVERSION –
A CHANGE OF LIFE

"For we are his workmanship, created in
Christ Jesus unto good works, which
God hath before ordained that we should
walk in them" (Ephesians 2:10).

I have showed you the work of conversion on your mind and on
your heart. The next thing to show you is the change it makes in your
life. The same God who requires the cleansing of your heart also
requires the cleansing of your life. He does not make us new
creations to do nothing, or to continue serving Satan. He makes us
new persons for a new work – to serve the living God (cf. I
Thessalonians 1:9). "For we are his workmanship, created in Christ
Jesus unto good works" (Ephesians 2:10).

It is only bragging to say you are converted if you keep on living
like you did before. Neither God nor man will believe you, although
you may deceive yourself. Since a new heart produces a new life, let
us think about that new life.

1. *The first change in the life is made up of the contract
   the converted person makes with Christ.* What has
   happened in your heart is now spoken with your mouth.
   "For with the heart man believeth unto righteousness;
   and with the mouth confession is made unto salvation"
   (Romans 10:10). A converted heart will produce a
   converted tongue; it will lead you to witness about your
   conversion both to God and to others.

   There might have been hypocritical promises before,
   which were soon broken from lack of sincerity, but
   conversion brings you into a true and lasting contract
   with Jesus Christ.

Before conversion, although Christ has been offered to you a thousand times, your dull mind did not take the gospel seriously, and would not come to Jesus so you could have life (cf. John 5:40). But when you are drawn by the Father, you will be glad to be united with Christ. When this happens you will be married to Him – in union with Him.

Have you come to this point? Have you taken Christ as He is offered to you? Have you given yourself to Him? Conversion will bring you into this agreement, this contract, with Christ. This contract is the whole basis of your change. It is explained in these words: "The union between Christ and you." This union with Him will cause you to openly confess Christ to the world. You will be quite willing to let lost people know that you are in agreement with Christ and not with them.

In this same contract, you will renounce all competitors to Christ. Before, you served other masters. But now you will serve only Christ. You will no longer try to serve both God and mammon, the Spirit and the flesh. Christ and Satan are as incompatible as light and darkness. It is the purpose of Christ to bring people out of captivity to Satan and sin (Acts 26:18; II Timothy 2:25-26). God teaches the sinner that there is no possibility of joining these together: either Satan or Christ must be given up. Either sin or salvation must be chosen. Either let sin go, or let Heaven go.

When the sinner lets go of sins, turns away from the world, determines that Christ alone shall be his Saviour, and actually comes to Christ to have his sins cleansed, he has moved into conversion. Every root of sin is destroyed in this one act, but especially the sin that lies behind all the rest – self-love and self-seeking. Every unconverted person lives for himself and seeks things that please himself alone. The carnal self is the great enemy that Christ must subdue in conversion. This is the great idol in every unconverted person that must be broken down — or there is no salvation.

The very nature of conversion is turning from self to Christ. Therefore, turning from sin to Christ is the *very thing* sinners should be seeking when they want to be converted.

Many a person has gone quite far, and seems to have renounced sin and come to Christ, who has shamefully fallen away in the end because he was not brought to a place of self-denial in a genuine conversion.

It is the love of carnal self which leads some people to sinful lusts, some people to ambitious ways, and others to fall back into the cares of this world, and so prove that they were unconverted in the end. Therefore you must denounce the love of self to be truly converted. When love of self is turned from, in conversion, three great master-sins are subdued: pride, covetousness, and voluptuousness. The destruction of these three sins is one half of the work of conversion. And the other half is turning to Jesus Christ fully.

2. When a sinner has made a contract like this with Christ, the next thing he must do is *actually turn away from the sin he has renounced.* Otherwise he has made a false promise, and this will not result in conversion. Before conversion all promises are so weakly made that they quickly vanish and the hearts of such people are as changeable as the moon. But when they are converted, they become men and women who keep their word, and mean what they say.

O what a sudden change appears in the lives of people when God has thoroughly done His work. I know this change of heart is His greatest work. It reflects in the convert's life. *People are often greatly surprised when they see the great change of a converted sinner's life.*

They are surprised because they do not know how God has worked in the convert's life to change it. They do not know of the fighting in his spirit between Christ and his flesh. Therefore, since they do not see the inner cause, the outer change of life seems very remarkable to them.

It is a miracle to see the effects of the power of Christ, and how suddenly the change in the convert often comes.

Take a man who has some slight convictions and half-repentance. See how long it takes him to reform. If he is used to some sin, he will not suddenly leave it. He sometimes stays away from it, as though he were reformed, and sometimes he does it again, because he has not truly been changed. But when he is really converted, you will see him leave his sin all at once. He will flee from the things he once delighted in.

The hypocrite, on the other hand, may make a great confession of sin, but he will not decidedly cast it out. He secretly treats his sin as a friend, although he openly speaks against it as an enemy. He will not sincerely renounce it, and throw it out with a resolution never to do it again. O how sweetly does he roll it in his thoughts in secret, while he publicly frowns upon it with the severest countenance.

Before conversion we cannot convince sinners to give up their transgressions. We cannot get them to stop their drunkenness, or covetousness, uncleanness, or swearing. Sometimes, they will stop, and then again they will not. Sometimes they have a flash of conviction and clean up their lives for a while. But when the fear passes, you will see that it's really not a change of heart that has taken place. They will love their sin even more when they go back to it.

But conversion makes an everlasting enemy of sin. Away go former sinful customs, covetous practices, wicked speeches and proud actions, as Sarah threw Hagar and Ishmael out of her house, and would receive them no more.

When a preacher speaks to an unconverted person about the bitterness of sin and judgment for sin, the sinner thinks very little about what he heard. Therefore he goes on in his old ways. But when converting grace comes, it makes people taste the bitterness of sin for themselves. Then they turn away from it.

Grace brings in light from God, which shows the sinner what he did not see before – how he has a swarm of snakes under his shirt, and was playing with them at the edge of the pit of Hell. When he sees this, he feels it is time to take another path.

In the Bible this sort of change occurred many times when people were converted. In Acts 9 you will find that Paul stopped persecuting and never persecuted again. In Titus 3:3-5 we have an exact description of the change of life which happened to Paul and some of his friends when they were converted:

> "For we ourselves also were sometimes foolish, disobedient, deceived, serving divers lusts and pleasures, living in malice and envy, hateful, and hating one another. But after that the kindness and love of God our Saviour toward man appeared, Not by works of righteousness which we have done, but according to his mercy he saved us, by the washing of regeneration, and renewing of the Holy Ghost" (Titus 3:3-5).

No man who continues to live in his former sinful way is converted, whatever change of heart he may pretend to have.

> "Know ye not that the unrighteous shall not inherit the kingdom of God? Be not deceived: neither fornicators, nor idolaters, nor adulterers, nor effeminate, nor abusers of themselves with mankind, Nor thieves, nor covetous, nor drunkards, nor revilers, nor extortioners, shall inherit the kingdom of God. And such were some of you: but ye are washed, but ye are sanctified,

> but ye are justified in the name of the Lord Jesus,
> and by the Spirit of our God"
> (I Corinthians 6:9-11).

Here you see that true conversion makes a great change
in a person's life. You were such, but it is not so now.

When God mentions the conversion of His people, He
says concerning their past sins, "Thou shalt cast them
away...thou shalt say unto it, Get thee hence" (Isaiah
30:22). With hatred a converted sinner will say to his
former sin, *"Get thee hence. It is by you that I have
suffered and would have been lost forever. It is by you
that I have wronged God, and therefore get away from
me! Get thee hence! Get away from me!"*

This description of conversion is given in the book of
Ezekiel:

> "Then said I unto them, Cast ye away every man
> the abominations of his eyes, and defile not
> yourselves with the idols of Egypt: I am the Lord
> your God. But they rebelled against me, and
> would not hearken unto me: they did not every
> man cast away the abominations of their eyes,
> neither did they forsake the idols of Egypt: then I
> said, I will pour out my fury upon them, to
> accomplish my anger against them in the midst of
> the land of Egypt" (Ezekiel 20:7-8).

And in Romans, we are given a similar description of
conversion:

> "The night is far spent, the day is at hand: let us
> therefore cast off the works of darkness, and let us
> put on the armour of light. Let us walk honestly,
> as in the day; not in rioting and drunkenness, not
> in chambering and wantonness, not in strife and
> envying" (Romans 13:12-13).

Isaiah says the same thing:

> "Wash you, make you clean; put away the evil of
> your doings from before mine eyes; cease to do

evil; Learn to do well; seek judgment, relieve the oppressed, judge the fatherless, plead for the widow" (Isaiah 1:16-17).

And again, the prophet says:

"Seek ye the Lord while he may be found, call ye upon him while he is near: Let the wicked forsake his way, and the unrighteous man his thoughts: and let him return unto the Lord, and he will have mercy upon him; and to our God, for he will abundantly pardon" (Isaiah 55:6-7).

A hundred more such passages of Scripture could be quoted, all of them showing that *there is no true conversion of the heart if the sin of the life is not cast away.*

You can know whether you have an unconverted heart by this one test: in every converted person, the main bent and desire of his heart is against sin, and he is eager to destroy it. But with the lost this is not so.

Next, a converted soul has a new work to do. The convert has his heart set on a new goal. He will begin to pray right away. He will also have a new way of talking, since he has a new heart, "For out of the abundance of the heart the mouth speaketh" (Matthew 12:34).

A converted heart will result in a change of companions. People like being with those who are similar to themselves. Wicked and worldly people enjoy being with others who are also wicked and worldly. But they do not want to be close friends with a real Christian. This is even true in church. The lost members of the church enjoy being with each other, but they avoid close fellowship with those who are truly converted. You will notice this with both the old and the young in churches. The lost gather together and shy away from the real Christians.

But when converting grace comes, your thinking changes. You will no longer want to be with carnal people. You will now enjoy being with sincere Christians.

Another change that happens is that you become concerned about those who are unconverted. You will desire others to be as free from the Devil as you are! You will have a strong zeal for the conversion of others when you are converted.

When conversion comes it makes a person pity those who are misled by sin. That's the reason Christians trouble you so much about getting saved. You wish they would let you alone, but they won't do it because they care about you.

If you were drowning, wouldn't it be right to try to save you? So, it is right for Christians to try to rescue you from drowning in Hell-fire. If you are angry with them because they won't leave you alone, remember it's because they care about you that they speak to you concerning your salvation.

Many false ministers will leave you alone in your sin. They are unconverted or uncalled themselves. Since they have so little concern about their own souls, do not be surprised that they care little about yours. Other professing Christians may leave you alone because they don't want to anger you. But they are false Christians. How could a real Christian stand to see someone on the edge of eternal destruction and not do anything to help him?

CHAPTER SEVEN

THE NATURE OF CONVERSION –
A CHANGE OF AFFECTIONS

"They that are in the flesh cannot please
God. But ye are not in the flesh, but in
the Spirit, if so be that the Spirit of God
dwell in you..." (Romans 8:8-9).

In the fifth chapter we saw several changes that take place in a
person's heart at conversion. In this chapter I will explain another
change in the heart, the change of affections, or feelings, in a person
who experiences true conversion.

1. *The first feelings that change are love and hatred.*
   Before conversion your heart does not love spiritual
   things. It does not love inward holiness or a holy life.
   It does not love people who are holy. It does not love
   God Himself, since He is just and holy. Indeed, your
   unconverted heart has an inward dislike, an aversion, to
   God and His ways. Unconverted people are usually so
   self-deceived, however, that they don't know this about
   themselves.

   The unconverted heart, instead of loving the things of
   God, loves pleasure and earthly profit, and the honor of
   this world. It really loves only these things (Romans
   8:5).

   But conversion will turn your love into hatred. It will
   make you love a holy God, and His holy people, and
   their way of living, which you could not love before,
   and makes you hate the sins which you enjoyed so
   much in the past. Conversion changes your loves and
   hatreds.

This is true in all real conversions. It can be seen in the following verses:

> "He that loveth father or mother more than me is not worthy of me" (Matthew 10:37).

> "In whose eyes a vile person is contemned; but he honoureth them that fear the Lord" (Psalm 15:4).

> "We know that we have passed from death unto life, because we love the brethren. He that loveth not his brother abideth in death" (I John 3:14).

> "And this is the condemnation, that light is come into the world, and men loved darkness rather than light, because their deeds were evil. For every one that doeth evil hateth the light, neither cometh to the light, lest his deeds should be reproved. But he that doeth truth cometh to the light, that his deeds may be made manifest, that they are wrought in God" (John 3:19-21).

Unconverted people hated the light before, because it was against their sins. But when converting grace comes, they will love it and come to it. On the other hand, the evil actions that they do, they will hate (Romans 7:15). Yes, they will hate even the garments spotted by the flesh (Jude 23). This means that when they are converted they will hate anything that bears the marks of a sinful life.

2. *The second two affections that change are desire and aversion (what you like and what you don't like).* These are similar to love and hatred – so I don't need to say too much about them. Unconverted people desire sensual things, which they love. They can never have enough of these things. The covetous man can never have enough money. The ambitious man can never have enough prestige. The sensualist can never be satisfied. Their whole lives thirst for the things of the flesh (Romans 13:14), and fulfilling its desires (Ephesians 2:3).

But concerning God, and church, and Heaven they have no appetite. They are naturally against these things, and at best only accept them coldly. This is why they reject all efforts to get them converted. If someone tries to make them think about spiritual things, there is a feeling inside them that is against it, so they will not listen.

This is why our work as ministers does so little good. If lost people had as much desire for Christ as they have for worldly things, think how quickly and easily they would be converted!

But when converting grace comes, it will change your desires. It will leave a secret thirst for Jesus in your soul. Then you will cry out with David, "My soul thirsteth after thee, as a thirsty land" (Psalm 143:6). Then the desire of your soul will be for Christ. You will see that He is more to be desired than gold, yea, than fine gold (Psalm 19:10).

Before, you desired many things, and nothing satisfied you. Now you want only one thing – Jesus – and you'll be fulfilled when you find Him (Psalm 27:4; 73:25).

3. *The next two affections changed in conversion are delight and sorrow.* Unconverted people naturally find no pleasure in God or spiritual things. "A fool hath no delight in understanding" (Proverbs 18:2). Sensual pleasure is what they desire (Titus 3:3), and the pleasures "of sin for a season" that they wish for (Hebrews 11:25). They live in pleasure on the earth, and fatten themselves for the day of slaughter (James 5:5). They not only do evil, but also enjoy being with those who do it (Romans 1:32). These "scorners delight in their scorning, and fools hate knowledge" (Proverbs 1:22).

But when converting grace comes, it will give you desires you never had before. Then the things that

76

seemed boring to you will become interesting. God Himself will be enjoyed by you (Psalm 40:8). On Sunday you will actually *prefer* worshipping Him in church to anything else! This will be no hardship to you, because you will *love* worshipping God when you are converted.

The wicked think they will never have a day of enjoyment again if they become Christians, but they will actually enjoy themselves more after they are converted than they *ever* did before! The enjoyment true Christians have in the things of God is greater than everything they had before.

The same is true of the *sorrow* of the converted. It is not the same as it was before conversion. It once caused them great pain to lose any pleasure, or to be wronged, or to suffer disgrace from people, or to lose something, or to experience bodily pain. They were actually the way Satan falsely accused Job of being. If you took anything away from them, they would have cursed God. But the fact that they were unconverted did not bother them at all. They were far more concerned about small things in this world than about their everlasting souls.

But it is completely different when conversion comes. Then they will weep over their sins, and cry because of their wickedness in the sight of God. They were not in tears over their sins before, but they will be when converting grace comes. Although they were not sorrowful over missing Heaven before, now they will be so full of sorrow over sin that they will turn away from it. They will do all they can to stop their sins when converting grace has come to them.

4. *The next affections which are changed in conversion are hope and despair.* Before conversion the minds of the lost are either lifted up by false hopes, or else they

fall into despair. The hopes of unconverted people show the self-delusion of their souls, and lead to eternal destruction.

As a person imagining he is going to London, who is actually going in the opposite direction, so these people commonly hope to get to Heaven while they are travelling on the road to Hell. Although God has told them that they will not have peace if they travel this road (Isaiah 59:8), and has assured them that there is no peace for the wicked (Isaiah 57:21; 48:22), yet they do not believe God; they go on hoping to find peace while living a wicked life. These deceiving hopes are the cause of eternal damnation for millions, as the Bible frequently tells us.

But when converting grace comes, it breaks down the deceptions of sinners, and makes them see how they have been tricked by Satan. It makes them see that all the things they trusted in were false hopes that could not save them.

When you are awakened by converting grace you will say, *"I once hoped to go to Heaven without conversion, but now I see that it can't be. I once hoped to be good enough. But now I realize that I deceived myself. I once hoped to be saved by Christ even though I loved the world and my sins. But now I see that I was a blind fool. I once thought I would be saved if I died, but now I see that I would have been lost forever."*

When you are first awakened you will be brought into a condition of despair. You will realize that you can never get to Heaven without conversion, and that you'll never be saved if you keep on thinking the way you do.

And then a new kind of hope will come, that you never had before. You will turn your hopes toward God and Christ. Now your hope will be built on Scriptures and on Jesus Christ Himself! Your hope will be built, then, on Jesus' Blood!

5. ***The next two affections changed in conversion are courage and fear.*** Unconverted people sin boldly, but have no fear of the wrath of God and Hellfire. These poor blind people are so courageous in their wickedness that they dare to sin, while those who are converted dare not. They dare to miss church, drink, tell dirty stories, have lost friends, commit other sins, and think little of God. They dare to risk the wrath of God and Hell itself. If you tell them these things, it has no effect on them whatever. In their insane courage, they dare to destroy their own souls. Like a psychologically unbalanced lunatic, who dares to leap in the water and drown himself, or a blind man, who dares to go down a dangerous mine-shaft, because he cannot see the great danger, so unconverted people have insane courage to continue in their lost condition.

But in doing what is right, they are cowards. They will not go through the slightest suffering now to prevent eternal suffering later. They are not willing to have any person even slightly make fun of them over Christianity and church attendance. Yet they have no concern at all about whether God is displeased with them. If they have some thought about becoming Christians, a wicked man can easily tease and laugh them out of it. Unconverted people do not dare to stand up against the mocking of their lost relatives and lost friends, the weakest enemies of Christianity. Yet they boldly risk the flames of Hell on a daily basis. This is common among unconverted people.

But when converting grace comes, you will be affected in the exact opposite way. Then you will be afraid of God and His displeasure, and very courageous against the opposition of lost acquaintances and relatives. You will then think it is insanity, not courage, to be fearless of the wrath of God. No one can stand against an all-powerful God, if He is against you. Therefore, in conversion, a person lays himself at the feet of God and says, "Lord, what wilt thou have me to do?" (Acts 9:6). *This is the reason that converts in Bible times often came trembling to Christ (Acts 16:29; 9:6). Trembling and fear of God's anger have always accompanied true revivals throughout history. The Bible says, "The fear of the Lord is the beginning of wisdom" (Psalm 111:10; Proverbs 1:7; 9:10).* In conversion you would not dare to do what you did before. You would have cursed and sworn, but now you don't dare. You would have secretly deceived and tricked other Christians, but now you don't dare. You would have committed other secret sins, because no one saw you, but now you don't dare do so, because you fear God who is greater than all. Now if you are tempted to sin, you think, "How then can I do this great wickedness, and sin against God?" (Genesis 39:9). By "fear of the Lord, men depart from evil" (Proverbs 16:6). It is the work of conversion to bring hardened sinners to fear God.

When you are converted you will have comparatively little fear of the threats of men, worldly losses, or anything else that stands in the way of getting to Heaven! Those who are truly converted have very little fear of these things. Here, where the lost are most cowardly, the converted soul is most courageous. The converted person will say, "The Lord is on my side; I will not fear: what can man do unto me?" (Psalm 118:6). "In God have I put my trust: I will not be afraid what man can do unto me" (Psalm 56:11). "Fear ye not the reproach of men, neither be afraid of their revilings. For the moth shall eat them up like a garment, and the worm shall eat them like wool: but my righteousness shall be for ever, and my salvation from generation to generation" (Isaiah 51:7,8).

When God changes people in conversion, He makes them soldiers under the flag of Christ, and sends them to fight against principalities and powers – the demons of this world. God therefore gives great courage to those who are converted. *The reason we see so little courage among church people today is that only a few of them have been converted. Make sure you are one of that small number!*

"Fear not, little flock; for it is your Father's good pleasure to give you the kingdom" (Luke 12:32).

6. *The next passion which changes in conversion is anger.* This is a single passion and has no opposite. Before conversion, people are angry with those who confront them with their sins. If you speak to those who are lost about the sins they love, they become very upset with you, as if you did them some deadly harm. You cannot even speak to them softly about their sins without them taking great offence, as if you were out to disgrace and destroy them!

If we do only half of our duty as ministers, when we show people that they are lost, they are highly offended at us, as if we said too much. When I consider what Heaven and Hell are, that one of them will be at the end of every person's life, my conscience tells me that I should be very earnest with lost sinners, and take no excuse from them, until they turn to Jesus Christ in full conversion.

They will say you are too zealous and too narrow if you are that earnest with them. But aren't those the same things the Pharisees said about Jesus Christ? Christ Himself is an offence to the ungodly world (I Peter 2:8; Romans 9:33). It is no wonder then if we who are converted to Christ also offend them. They will bear a secret grudge in their minds against a Christian who troubles them in their sins. "Anger resteth in the bosom of fools" (Ecclesiastes 7:9).

If you came in and turned the lights on, and caught a thief or an adulterer, he would be offended. So wicked people are offended when a minister points out their sins.

But when converting grace comes, you will have a change of heart. You will then thank the preacher you were angry with. You will not love anyone more than you love the person who cared for your soul. A special love to those who were the means of your conversion will remain in your heart forever. You will be like an insane man who fought with his doctor, and treated those who tried to cure him as if they came to kill him. But when he returns to his right mind, he will thank the doctors with all his heart. A sinner, before his conversion, is displeased with those who try to help him – but when God turns his heart he will deeply love those who brought him to Christ.

When you are converted, your anger will turn away from others and will be turned against yourself. You were never so irritated at the preacher for reproving you as you will be at yourself for sinning against God. *There is in every converted person a great self-anger, an indignation against himself because of his sin.* You will say, "I have sinned greatly" (II Samuel 24:10). Paul himself says he was insane! "Exceedingly mad against" the Christians before his conversion (Acts 26:11). And of himself and some other people, he said, "We ourselves also were sometimes foolish, disobedient, deceived, serving divers lusts and pleasures, living in malice and envy, hateful, and hating one another" (Titus 3:3). So you see that converted people are angry with themselves for their sinfulness. Every converted sinner hates himself for his iniquity. This is why a real convert easily denies himself, while a false convert will not. *False converts fall back into nominal Christianity because they have never been brought to hate themselves and their sinfulness. They have been forgiven little, so they love little (Luke 7:47).* Therefore, they easily fall back into sin and nominal Christianity, because their conversion was false in the first place (Luke 8:13-14).

7. *The last change in the affections made by converting grace is in the area of man's content and discontent.* Before you are converted, you are discontented if you do not have worldly pleasures. It is in the things of this world that lost people find satisfaction and happiness. But they think they can do just as well without spiritual things.

Conversion changes the heart also on these matters. A lost person is troubled and restless if his friends, or his house, or his health or something else in this world is not just right. He is unhappy because he looks for contentment on this earth. Therefore he is troubled when he loses earthly joys.

A true convert, on the other hand, is troubled more by spiritual things than physical. If God hides His face, if the Spirit appears to withdraw, if there is trouble between him and a brother in the church, he is deeply pained. Nothing will make him feel better until these things are resolved. He is like a child who will not be quieted by anything except that which it cries for. So, the true Christian is not content with anything in the world except Christ Himself. The true convert is content with what he has, because God has promised that He will never leave him nor forsake him (Hebrews 13:5).

Comments on Matthew 18:3

"Except ye be converted, and *become as little children*, ye shall not enter into the kingdom of heaven" (Matthew 18:3).

Christ does not mean that children are sinless, or free from the threat of Hell. This is what the verse means:

83

1. At conversion you begin anew, like a child. You begin your life anew – born again! You start a new life when you are converted, as a child has a new life to live.

2. At conversion you become as a little child in humility and in seeking small things. Children do not think of gaining wealth or of becoming independent and free of responsibility. Their minds are too simple for these things, and so your mind will be when you are converted. It is as impossible to become a true Christian without humility as it is for a house to stand without a foundation.

CHAPTER EIGHT

AN APPEAL TO THE UNCONVERTED

"Why will ye die?" (Ezekiel 33:11).

I come to you in the name of Jesus Christ. My concern is your salvation. I know that very soon we will be in another world, and we will all meet at the day of Judgment. My purpose is to prepare you for that day. I have not tried to please you. I have not given you funny stories or novel doctrines. I hope you will pardon my bluntness when you realize that you are lost. Then you will see that my business as a pastor is to lead you to conversion.

I hate preaching that only "tickles the ears" and leaves the hearer unconcerned and unconverted. If the town were on fire, it wouldn't be right to play the violin and dance. The right thing to do would be to *put out* the fire! If I saw you sinking in a broken ship, ready to drown if you had no help, it would not be right for me to give you a great speech. I should be helping you to escape from danger instead!

That's why I come to help you out of your unconverted state. I see your destruction right in front of you – and I come in the name of God, and call on you to take a stand now, and go no farther in your wickedness.

Don't wait any longer. Turn from your sins to Jesus Christ. Remember, if you do not believe on Christ, you will be ruined. "For if ye live after the flesh, ye shall die" (Romans 8:13).

What do you say? *Will you* turn to Christ from the lusts of the flesh, the love of the world, and a careless, ungodly life – or will you *refuse* to do that? Let your answer be "yes" or "no." Will you turn to Christ and be converted? – or will you refuse and die in your sins? Do any of you dare to say "no"? I hope not! But it is the same as saying "no" if you say nothing. Don't tell me that you hope to be saved some day – with a cold look on your face! A thousand decisions like this, without emotion, have left souls to perish in endless terror. You must have a very strong desire to be converted.

What do you say? Will you turn, or won't you? Be careful what you say – because God is present and sees your heart! Do not stand still between two opinions! If Baal (Satan) be God, follow him – if your sinful friends be God, follow them – but if the Lord be God, follow Him! (I Kings 18:21).

Don't tell me you're going to wait until tomorrow, or some time after that. This always means that you want to keep sinning a little longer. No promise that you will search for Christ is honest unless you mean to do it *now!* The person who will not come to Christ today will probably *never* do it! No one who loves God wants to put off being reconciled to Him. Do it *now* – if you are serious! Stop fooling with God. A person who wants to keep his sins for one night will keep them a year, seven years, and forever – if he can. If you will not come to Christ now, you will probably never do it. To help you determine your answer, here are some serious questions.

1. *What do you think would have happened to you if you had died before conversion?* Where do you think you would be right now if you had died last week? If you had died unconverted a month ago, where would you be today? You say that you don't know? Well, what does the Bible say? Do you know that? Concerning the unconverted, God says He will "cast them into a furnace of fire: there shall be wailing and gnashing of teeth" (Matthew 13:42).

How easily God could have killed you last week. He could have taken your life by choking you to death on your food. He could have struck you down by letting your foot slip, by an accident, besides many hundreds of diseases. You would have died, and your unconverted soul would have sunk down into the flames of another world.

You can't really imagine how terrible it is for an unconverted soul to appear suddenly in front of God. Many people are frightened by the thought of death. But think farther – what it will feel like to suddenly be ejected from your body into a black world of fallen angels, undying worms, and burning fire, with demons screaming and gnawing on you – and no water to drink! It is everlasting torment, which should upset you. Oh, friend, think of the horrible state you would have been in if you had died a few days ago without being converted! God says to you just what he said to Lot:

"Escape for thy life; look not behind thee..." (Genesis 19:17).

That is the warning I give you – *"Escape for your life! Look not behind you! Do not stay in your sins any longer, or you will perish. You will be cut off if you wait."*

That is my first question: What would have happened to you if you had already died without being converted?

2. *My next question is, Are you sure if you wait another day, that you will be kept out of Hell that day?* If you refuse the salvation Christ offers you now, are you certain you will live another day? Are you sure that your body won't be at the morgue and your soul in Hell before you have another chance to be converted?

You are not sure of it. If you say you are sure, let's see your evidence. Has God promised you anywhere in the Bible another day of life? Can you live a day without the help of God? You know you can't. You know that many who were as strong as you are now dead. They didn't fear death either. Now they *are* dead – their souls in Hell. You must die also. The thought should be constantly in your mind, "What will happen to me if I die tonight?" Christ said,

"Except ye be converted, and become as little children, ye shall not enter into the kingdom of heaven" (Matthew 18:3).

Every night when you lie down in bed you should think, "What if I die in an unconverted state before morning?" When you get up the next day, you should think, "What if I die in an unconverted state before night?" The daily thoughts of dying without being converted should stop you from laughing and take away all enjoyment from you. *How can you stand to be in such danger?*

You say, "Well, I have lived many days already, and I will most likely live another day." I answer – but who would gamble like this on his eternal salvation? You are gambling with your soul! "The Bible says, "Boast not thyself of to morrow: for thou knowest not what a day may bring forth" (Proverbs 27:1).

3. *My third question is, What do you think is best, Heaven or earth, a life in glory or the present pleasures of sin?* Are you *sure* that it is better to be drunk than sober, better to live in sin than to live for God? Is *this* what you believe? If it is, you are a heathen and not a Christian. In fact, you are worse than most heathens in the world. If this is not what you believe, how dare you live as though it were? Will you act against your own knowledge? Won't you do what you know is pleasing to God and best for yourself? Who can help you if you know that the way you are going leads to death, and yet you go on that way – and refuse to be converted? *Who will pity you if you willingly destroy yourself?*

But when converting grace comes, it gives you desires you never had before. Then the things that seemed uninteresting to you, and boring to you before, will become delightful and enjoyable. God Himself will be enjoyed by you (Psalm 40:8). On Sunday you will *love* worshipping Him in church. This will not seem hard to you, because you will *love* it when you are converted.

4. *My fourth question is, Do you believe humans were made for this world only, or for a better world in Heaven?* If you desire to go to Heaven aren't you foolish not to do everything possible to get there? If Heaven can be reached, aren't you a fool if you do not try to reach it? Do you think you were made only for

this earth, and that when you die there is nothing else? If you think that, you are more ignorant than a heathen.

God made three kinds of beings. One kind is completely spirit. Some are angels, and others sinned and became demons. Another kind is pure flesh, animals and birds, without immortal spirits. The third kind is the humans, which have spirits and flesh. Man, with his spirit, has a soul which lives endlessly. Animals do not know there is another life. They do not live in hope or fear of eternity as we do. Experience shows that unconverted people fear only physical death. But those who are awakened by God fear the second death – eternal torment in Hell.

If humans were made for Heaven, isn't it right to seek Heaven and live for it? Remember that conversion causes you to think about the place you were made for – Heaven. Conversion makes you feel like a human rather than an animal. It makes you live like a human being instead of a beast. Sin makes us like animals. But conversion restores our humanity, and makes us live for Heaven – the place we were created for. If you believe that humans are more than animals, if you believe we were made for Heaven, get rid of worldly sins! *Live as though you are just passing through this world on the way to everlasting life!*

5. My next question to you is, *have you ever thought about the gain and the loss connected with conversion?* Did you ever think about the peace and everlasting glory which come to those who are converted, and the misery and horror that come to those who neglect salvation? Surely if you had thought very much about the gain and the loss, you would have been much more interested in conversion than you have been until now. Sinner, when God and His preachers tell you to be converted, but year after year you are still the same, there is something wrong with you. You must be afraid of giving up a sin you enjoy. Otherwise, why do

you put off conversion? I ask you, is there anything better than the salvation of your soul?

What are you afraid of losing by being converted? Is it anything worth keeping? What is it you are not willing to give up? Is it your sins, your sinful pleasures, your "freedom" – which of these? Isn't it sad that you are not willing to come to Christ for fear of losing some passing pleasure? If you think this world is better than God, if you are afraid of turning to Christ for fear of being a loser, there is nothing I can do for you. You will have to wait for death before you see what a fool you were.

6. My next question to you is, ***have you got any good reason not to seek your conversion now?*** Do you have any reason for not seeking Christ and being converted? Don't pass by this question thoughtlessly. Give me your answer. Have you got a reason for rejecting conversion or don't you? If you have no reason, your own conscience tells you that you are not converted simply because of your ***lazy neglect.*** You do not turn to Christ simply because ***you will not turn to Him.***

How dare you put off your conversion? If sin seems good to you, isn't holiness better? Aren't pardon, and hope, and peace, and Heaven better than sin? Will you be able to use your love of sin as an excuse for not being converted when you stand before God at the Judgment?

7. My next question is, ***have you ever thought about who is in favor of your conversion and who is against it?*** You have already seen who is for it: God is for it, the Christians in Heaven are for it, the preachers of the gospel are for it, and every real Christian on earth is for it. God is so much in favor of it that He sent His Son to die to purchase it for you (John 3:16). God pleads with you, and asks you, "Why will you die?" (Ezekiel 33:11). Jesus is so much in favor of your salvation that He made it His whole work. He became a man,

suffered the curse of the Cross, sent His ministers to proclaim it, and prays for it now in Heaven. The Holy Spirit is for your conversion. That is why He pricks your conscience. The Christians who are already in Heaven are for it. That is why they rejoice when a sinner repents. The preachers of the gospel are for it. That is why they preach to you!

But who is *against* your conversion? Satan is against it. The demons are against it. Other unconverted people, who are under the power of Satan, are against it. Your own wicked and depraved nature is against it.

I say that there is no one in the world except Satan, demons, sinful people, and your own wicked nature, who are against your conversion. If these are the ones you listen to, your own conscience should tell you that you are a fool.

8. I have a few more questions to ask you. My next one is this: *Would you rather die in a converted or in an unconverted condition?* In which of these two states would you rather die? Remember, you *will* either die converted or unconverted. Which would you rather have at the end of life? I hope you will be very serious as you answer this question. I ask you, which of these two conditions would you rather be in at the time of your death? If you said, "I would rather be converted," then why not *now?* If you would rather be converted at the time of your death, then seek conversion quickly. Otherwise death may come unexpectedly, and catch you unprepared. Also, remember that the Holy Spirit may leave you. If you commit the unpardonable sin, and the Holy Spirit leaves you, you are doomed while you live! Therefore, you are a fool not to seek conversion now!

9. My next question is this: *If God sent an angel from Heaven to you to tell you to be converted, would you listen to him and obey him or not?* If an angel came and appeared to you and told you to turn to Christ now, what would you do? What answer would you give the

angel? Would you tell him, "I will not be converted. I would rather live my life in sin"? Would you say that to him? Surely you wouldn't dare to do that, would you? Wouldn't you say, "Yes, I am sorry for my sins. I will turn from them to Christ right now"? Wouldn't you say that if an angel came and spoke to you about your salvation?

Yet the Bible is a better witness than any angel. And God has given the Bible, which says,

> "Except ye be converted, and become as little children, ye shall not enter into the kingdom of heaven" (Matthew 18:3).

If you say you would listen to an angel, shouldn't you listen even more to the Bible, which is the Word of God? Shouldn't you listen to the preachers God has sent you? Shouldn't you listen to the promptings of the Holy Spirit in your heart? If conversion is a doctrine you would receive from an angel, tell me why you don't receive it from the Word of God, from His preachers, and from the Holy Spirit?

10. The last question that I will ask you is this: *Will you have any excuse for not being converted when you stand before God at the Last Judgment?* Will you have any excuse when you stand before God? Or will you be left speechless and under the condemnation of your own conscience for ever? Is it wrong for God to throw out the people who threw themselves away? Is it wrong for God to throw you out of Heaven when no sermon will move you, and no amount of reasoning will satisfy you?

You will realize that you ruined *yourself* in that day. God will say, "What could have been done more to my vineyard, that I have not done in it?" (Isaiah 5:4). "What more could I have said to this sinner than I have said?"

What excuse for staying unconverted *will* you have at the Last Judgment?

Dear friend, I have begged you to be converted so you can live. I have meant you no harm, unless salvation is a harm! The threatenings of the Bible, and the horrible state of unconverted souls were all true before I ever lived, and before I ever wrote this book.

Have I convinced you to be converted or haven't I? Do you intend to be converted or not?

Jesus says to you:

> "Come unto me...and I will give you rest" (Matthew 11:28).

Will you come to Jesus or not?

In conclusion I say this: If you stand before God at the Judgment in an unconverted state, after all the warnings I have given you, I hope that God will not blame me, who faithfully tried to prevent it.

CHAPTER NINE

DELIBERATE NEGLECT OF THE MEANS GOD HAS GIVEN

"Incline your ear, and come unto me: hear,
and your soul shall live" (Isaiah 55:3).

By this time I hope you are willing to be converted, and are ready to ask what you can do to experience it. Therefore I will show you the common obstacles to conversion, which you must remove or overcome. I will also give you the corresponding directions to follow.

Hindrance Number One. The first obstacle to conversion is the deliberate neglect of the means God has given to bring it about.

1. ***The first thing God uses to bring about conversion is hearing sermons in church.***

> "How shall they believe in him of whom they have not heard? And how shall they hear without a preacher?...So then faith cometh by hearing, and hearing by the word of God" (Romans 10:14, 17).

God sent Paul to open men's eyes and convert them (Acts 26:17-18). God sent an angel to Cornelius, not to preach the gospel, but to direct him to a human ***preacher***, because God wanted to do things in the usual way, and have a ***preacher*** speak to the lost man (Acts 10:3-5). This is why Christ stopped Paul in a vision, and yet sent him to Ananias for instruction (Acts 9:6-10). It was by hearing Peter preach that the Jews were converted, and three thousand were added to the church all at once (Acts 2:37-41). It was God who opened the heart of Lydia, but why did He open it? He opened her heart to listen carefully to the things that were spoken by Paul, so she could be converted (Acts 16:14). God sent an earthquake to prepare the heart of the jailor, but He did not convert him without the *preaching* of Paul and Silas (Acts 16:32). If people will not hear *preachers*, the *preachers* must shake the dust off of their feet in witness against them (Matthew 10:14). And Christ said it will be more tolerable for Sodom and Gomorrah at the Last Judgment than for such people. It is by *preachers* that Christ teaches His churches (Ephesians 4:11). Every person who refuses to hear will be cut off from His people (Acts 3:23).

If you stay at home when the sermon is given, you will not be helped by it. *If you find something else do to when you should hear the sermon, God will find something else to do when you need Him (Proverbs 1:28-29).*

If you think you can read the Bible and be saved without going to church to hear the preacher, isn't this *horrible pride* in you – to think you are able to understand the Word of God as well without a preacher as with one? When Philip asked him whether he understood what he read, the wise eunuch said to him, "How can I, except some man should guide me?" (Acts 8:30-31), and yet you think you can read the Bible and be saved without a preacher!

Would your children be right to say, *"We have the same books at home, therefore we won't go to school. Our teacher only instructs us in these books. We can read them for ourselves at home"* – would they be right to say that? And are you wiser than God, who sent His preachers? (Ephesians 4:11-16). If you say you don't need to hear the preacher, you must indeed think you are smarter than God, who sent the preacher to guide you.

Look through the Bible and see whether or not the usual way of conversion in Bible times was by hearing preachers.

By missing church you excommunicate yourself! You cut yourself off from the communion, the fellowship of the saints, the visible body of Christ. You cut yourself off from the preaching that could have converted you.

The sixth council at Constantinople (AD 680) declared that whoever was absent from the congregation three Lord's-days together without a good reason, if he were a minister, would be expelled from the ministry, and if he were a layman, he would be excluded from the communion of the church, dropped from its membership and privileges.

Dr. Hymers' note: How much stronger would our churches be today if they followed the example of these ancient Christians? They would be smaller – but a great deal stronger and more Biblical.

2. ***Another thing God uses to bring about conversion is reading the Bible.*** Although this must not replace church attendance, where you hear the preaching of the Word, it is an excellent means of grace, or God would not have told us to read it. "The law of the Lord is perfect, converting the soul" (Psalm 19:7). It is a great privilege to have the verses on the page before our eyes, so we can read them over until they enter our hearts.

3. ***Another thing God uses to bring about conversion is listening seriously to those God sent to teach us.*** Nicodemus came to Jesus by night for counsel, because he knew that Christ was a teacher sent from God. And Jesus gave him advice concerning the new birth. Another asked what he should do to have eternal life (Matthew 19:16). The eunuch asked Philip to teach him (Acts 8:31). Paul asked Ananias, and Cornelius asked Peter, as I said before. The Jews who were pricked in the heart asked Peter and the rest of the Apostles what they should do (Acts 2:37). The jailor asked Paul and Silas what he should do to be saved (Acts 16:30).

96

If unconverted sinners would follow these examples, and go to the preacher for direction regarding their salvation, and decide to do exactly what the preacher says, conversions would not be so rare, and so many mistakes would not be made. But most persons are so careless that they feel no need to go to the preacher. Others are so proud that they will not humble themselves and do it. Others think they already know what the preacher will say, and so they do not ask for his counsel. Thus Satan keeps people from salvation by keeping them from their preachers, from this means of grace.

4. *Another thing God uses to bring about conversion is frequent fellowship with good Christians.* The friends you make have a transforming power, and the words and example of Christians do a great deal to make you think about your soul. Most people are much like their friends. The unconverted person should be in church at every service, to be around people who will help him to be converted.

5. *Another thing God uses to bring about conversion is frequent and earnest prayer to God.* When you know that you need grace, and that God is the one who gives it, what should you do? You should ask God for saving wisdom and grace (James 1:5). I know some people teach that those who are unconverted should not pray, because without faith they cannot please God. But the Bible commands unconverted men to pray: "Seek ye the Lord while he may be found, call ye upon him while he is near: Let the wicked forsake his way, and the unrighteous man his thoughts" (Isaiah 55:6-7; Hosea 10:12; Amos 5:6). Peter told the unconverted Simon Magus to pray (Acts 8:22-23).

So, hindrance (obstacle) number one is the deliberate neglect of the means God has given for the work of conversion. Now I give you the first direction, designed to remove this obstacle, which is: *you should use the means which God has appointed for your conversion.*

1. *Make sure that you are in every church service to hear the preaching.* Don't let anything but *extreme* necessity keep you from even one service. If you are absent without an extreme reason from even one sermon, God may justly deny you the blessing of the rest. Satan will be aware of what the preacher has been studying all week, and when he sees that he is going to preach what you need to hear, he may do his very best to keep you away from church that day. He may give you some excuse, or tempt you to miss, because he is afraid that if you come you will be converted. Therefore, do not miss one sermon, or you may miss the one that would have converted you.

   And as you listen to the sermons, be very careful *how* you listen. Christ often said, "He that hath ears to hear, let him hear." A person who does not listen carefully to the sermons doesn't deserve to have ears.

2. If you wish to be converted by the preaching of God's Word, *do not let the sermon slip from your mind as soon as you hear it. Think* about what you heard, and *speak* about it to those around you in the church. If your memory is too weak to remember, ask another Christian to repeat the main ideas of the sermon to you.

3. *Spend much time reading the Bible.* Think seriously about what you read.

4. *Especially do all this on Sundays.* When the church service is over, on Sundays, take time with your families or by yourselves, to go over the sermons you hear, to read the Bible, and pray. Seek knowledge about God on Sundays, if you wish to be converted by His grace. *Do not let work keep you from Sunday services. Before you take a job, tell your boss you will not work on Sundays. Flee from Sunday work, as Lot*

fled from Sodom. No amount of money is worth the loss of your soul.

5. *Go talk to your pastor regarding conversion.* Answer the pastor's questions, and decide beforehand that you will do what he says. Follow his advice carefully (Hebrews 13:17).

6. *Pray every day. Ask God to convert you.* Beg Him to open your eyes and show you your misery and sin until you are humbled. Ask God to make you hunger and thirst after Christ and His righteousness. Pray to God, with all your heart, that He would not let you remain unconverted any longer, or death may find you in a lost state. Beg God to forgive your former rebellion and resistance of His Spirit, and ask Him now to give you the grace which you have so long neglected. Ask Him to bring you to the place of hating the sinful pleasures you loved before. Ask Him to draw you to Christ for salvation.

These are the means God has given to bring you to salvation in Christ. Are you willing? Have you made up your mind to follow the advice I have given, and use the means God has appointed? Unless you are such a fool that you want to give up the joys of Heaven and endure the intolerable pains of Hell – then be serious about obeying what I have said, without waiting any longer!

CHAPTER TEN

HINDRANCES TO CONVERSION

"Who did hinder you that ye should not
obey the truth?" (Galatians 5:7).

The second hindrance to conversion is bad company. It is
dangerous to be a companion and friend with ungodly people. Even
if they don't say anything directly against what the Bible teaches, they
will do much to stop your salvation by keeping your thoughts and
conversation on other things, and by giving you an evil example, as if
eternal things were not necessary. Worldly talk and sinful actions
cause people's minds to neglect heavenly things. Also, lost friends
will tempt you to do things that oppose the work of the Holy Spirit,
and try to get you to sin, which produces damnation. *The noise of
their laughter and foolish talk will drown out the voice of your
conscience and of the Spirit of God. It is hard for a person to
concentrate on becoming a Christian if he is influenced by lost
people.*

O what a dangerous thing it is to have friendships with people
who are worldly or sensual, and are enemies of godliness. The Bible
says, "He that walketh with wise men shall be wise: but a companion
of fools shall be destroyed" (Proverbs 13:20).

Do all you can to avoid being with those who try to stop your
conversion, and make close friends with real Christians, who will
help you in the matter of your salvation. I do not mean that a small
child should leave ungodly parents or that a wife should leave her
ungodly husband. Your relations bind you in your place. But I mean
that no one should willingly be a friend of those who are not good
Christians. Choose the best Christians for friends. Live with those on
earth that you want to live with in Heaven.

"Be ye not unequally yoked together with unbelievers"
(II Corinthians 6:14).

"Wherefore come out from among them, and be ye
separate, saith the Lord...and I will receive you, And

100

will be a Father unto you, and ye shall be my sons and daughters, saith the Lord Almighty" (II Corinthians 6:17-18).

The next obstacle to conversion is ignorance of the truth. A person will not turn to Christ or turn away from sin without knowing who Christ is or what sin is. No one will go against his own nature and forsake the world, including the things he loves the most, until he knows why this is necessary, and knows about something better he can have by being converted.

Wickedness is loved because of ignorance. Even those who think they know these things, and yet remain unconverted, do not *really* know them, but only believe them as opinions, doctrines that they have never experienced themselves. The truth is that you must know the truths of Scripture by experience to be converted. The Bible says, "How shall they believe in him of whom they have not heard?" (Romans 10:14). "So then faith cometh by hearing, and hearing by the word of God" (Romans 10:17). "He that walketh in darkness knoweth not whither he goeth" (John 12:35).

Sinners would not play with sin if they really *knew* what they were doing. They would not run in crowds to eternal ruin, if they really *knew* that they were fools to do so.

If you want to be converted learn the way of salvation and the Scriptures which teach salvation. Only a knowledge of the Bible can get rid of darkness, because Satan haunts people in the night of ignorance. But if you listen to the light of Bible knowledge, the Devil will be gone. You need to (1) listen to sermons from the Word of God, (2) counsel with godly men, because they will teach you knowledge about salvation, and (3) read the Bible every day.

If you think you can be converted without knowledge, you have deceived yourself. God has made the way of salvation clear in the Bible, and He has sent you preachers and teachers, and many other things to help you. So you have no excuse if you remain ignorant. You can learn how to be a Christian even if you aren't a scholar. If you think you can be excused from this knowledge, you may as well think you can be excused from love and obedience, because you can't have either one of these without knowledge.

If you think you can be saved without knowing the basic truths of the Bible, you are deceived. Christ said, "This is life eternal, that they might know thee the only true God, and Jesus Christ, whom thou hast sent" (John 17:3). How can you have eternal life without this knowledge?

The next hindrance to conversion is unbelief. This means you won't be persuaded by the Word of God, but continue to doubt the things God has revealed in the Bible concerning eternity. Unconverted people only have a little knowledge of these truths, not enough to overcome their sinful desires.

You have three great enemies of the Christian faith. If you do not overcome them, you will lose your soul. They are,

1. Your own unbelieving heart, and sinfully depraved nature.

2. Satan, who trembles himself, but does all he can to stop you from believing.

3. Ungodly friends, who are used by Satan to keep you from being converted.

If you wish to be savingly converted, you must believe the Word of God. You must fully believe what the Bible says about everlasting happiness for the saved, and everlasting torment for the damned. To believe the Bible savingly you must do the following things:

1. Do not trust your own heart or your own thoughts. Your heart and mind are natural enemies of the Word of God. No wonder you don't believe it!

2. Do not think too highly of your own mind, as though you could easily understand the deep truths of the Bible.

3. Hate the first temptation of Satan, to doubt the Bible (Genesis 3:1). Get rid of these horrible thoughts and do not keep thinking about them.

4. Hate the company of unbelievers, who dare to speak against the Bible. Leave them right away when they say anything against the Scriptures.

5. Learn the Scriptures. Read the Bible daily and memorize verses that will help you.

6. Submit to the truth you know. Do not reject or neglect what you have already learned. Let the truth you learn affect your life and thinking.

By doing those six things you will do much to overcome your unbelief.

The next hindrance is inconsideration, thoughtlessness, indifference. The inconsiderate person is unconcerned, unmoved, lukewarm, dull, heedless, unmindful, incurious, insensible, unmindful, uninterested.

When the truths of salvation are not thought about carefully, they are like medicine which remains in the jar. The medicine will not help you unless you swallow it yourself! The truths of conversion must fill your mind and come down into your heart until you *feel* them.

You cannot expect the Word of God to convert you if you don't *think about* it with deep consideration. If you go to the best doctor in town, all he can do is give you medicine. It is up to you to *take* the medicine. Preachers tell you the truths that are most useful to your conversion, and if you will think deeply about what we say – especially after the services – and meditate on what we say when you are alone – until these truths sink into your heart – you may be converted. But if we can't get you to think deeply and seriously about these things when you are alone, how can we do you any good?

Have you ever seriously asked yourself whether you are converted or not? Have you ever thought of the blessedness of being converted, and the horrible misery of remaining unconverted? Have you thought about these things until they penetrated your heart? If you haven't, no wonder you are still unconverted! If you go to Hell, can you complain, knowing that I couldn't get you to think seriously about conversion? If conversion is not worth having, it is not worth thinking about very much. But if salvation isn't worth thinking about, I don't know what is!

The pastor does not go home with you after church. He does not see what you think about there when you are alone. He does not know if you kneel down before God and pray concerning the sermons you hear. The pastor does not know what you talk about to others.

But God follows you home. God sees and hears everything you do. God is ready to help you through what you heard in church if you do not reject it – by putting the sermons out of your mind after church is over. If you had really thought about who God is, what Christ has done for you, and what Heaven and Hell and death are, could you have remained unconverted? You would escape from your lost condition as you would from a house on fire over your head, or from a ship that is sinking!

> "I thought on my ways, and turned my feet unto thy testimonies. I made haste [hurried] and delayed not to keep thy commandments" (Psalm 119:59-60).

The next hindrance to conversion is hardness of heart and a seared conscience. Although everyone has some of this hardness before he is converted, yet the longer you resist conversion, the greater it becomes. When people sin for a long time and resist Christ over and over, they usually become senseless and "unreasonable men" (II Thessalonians 3:2).

Dr. Hymers' note: An old atheist who goes to my gym has the face of rebellion – against God. As I was swimming the other day, I noticed him lying in the sun by the pool, sleeping. Even while sleeping his face has the expression of rebellion. His rejection of God has gone on so long that it appears in the very look on his face – even when he's asleep! If you go on rejecting Christ, this rebellion will also become a part of your personality, making it increasingly difficult for you to be converted as time goes by.

People are born dead in sin by nature. But when they go on choosing to sin, they grow even more dead – that is, they become increasingly less sensitive, and have more death within themselves. As a dead body is fresh at the beginning, and doesn't appear to be dead when first laid out in the coffin – but rots after a time – and at last is nothing but a skeleton – so a sinner becomes increasingly spoiled and putrid if he remains in a state of death – by rejecting conversion.

When a person is finally so deeply ruined by spiritual death that God gives up on him, then a preacher can't say anything that will even touch him, because he is now so hard-hearted that he won't receive any of it.

Oh what sad work it is to deal with hardened hearts. It is like trying to plow a rock or swim through glue. Speaking to such hardened people troubles ministers greatly. It kills the minister's hopes, tires him out, and makes him say to himself, "I have worked without results, and spent my time and energy for nothing." This has broken the heart of many ministers. How horrible it is to see people a few days or years from eternal fire, which they could escape if they would wake up in time. But the pastor cannot get them to think seriously about it!

"Oh," thinks the pastor, *"if I could only awaken him, and make him care about his soul, I could prevent his damnation. The Bible is so clear that I think he would see the truth if he stopped closing off his mind. But I can't get him to think about these things! How sad! How pitiful! How discouraging!"*

Of all sorts of sinners, there are few that we have less hope for than those who are hard-hearted. Christ Himself was grieved with the hardness of their hearts (Mark 3:5). And when the Apostles preached the gospel of salvation, "divers were hardened, and believed not, but spake evil of that way before the multitude," until the Apostles resolved to leave them alone, without help (Acts 19:9).

I beg you to seek conversion through Christ now, before your heart becomes so hard that it is too late.

CHAPTER ELEVEN

HINDRANCES TO CONVERSION –
CONTINUED

"Who did hinder you that ye should not
obey the truth?" (Galatians 5:7).

*The seventh hindrance to conversion is allowing sin to become
a habit.* Our depraved natures produce strong sin, but habits make sin
even stronger. When sin becomes such a habit that you think you
have to keep doing it, it becomes the ruler of your mind.

When people have committed sins for a long time they become
hardened, as the hands of a gardener or a carpenter become thickened
with calluses. So sin becomes familiar to them; they go "past feeling"
and begin "to work all uncleanness with greediness" (Ephesians
4:19). When people get drunk or high on drugs, or commit other
horrible sins, it makes their consciences insensible. The next
temptation is yielded to more easily. By often sinning, people lose
their ability to tell right from wrong, or to feel guilty. Their hearts
become so hard that they feel they cannot live without the sin they
love so much. As a drug addict thirsts for more drugs, so they thirst
for the pleasures of the sins to which they have become addicted.
They feel that they **must** have these sins. It shouldn't surprise us that
habit in false religion, drunkenness, and other sins enslave people and
damn them to Hell. Sinful habits are a great obstacle to conversion.

You young people should be careful not to develop sinful habits.
If you already have such habits, you should take a strong stand
against them and go no farther in them. It is sad that you have gone
so far in sin already. But if you go on even one more day, God may
give up on you. If you add even one more sin to the heap, it may sink
you into Hell. Oh, how foolish it is for you to put off repentance,
when habits of sinning make it harder and harder to be converted as
time goes by.

Remember that the habit of sinning is no excuse. What if you
habitually spit in the face of your father? Would you make the excuse
of saying it was your habit to do so? The oftener you sin, the oftener

you rebel against God, and the more you should be sorrowful over it and stop doing it. What greater insanity can there be than to think you can be excused for sinning because it is your habit?

If you love sin because you are used to it, you will soon see whether you love Hell because you are used to it.

Hindrance number eight is foolish self love, which keeps you from judging yourself harshly enough, or makes you think you can be saved without being converted, or causes you to think you are converted when you're not. If you think you don't need to be converted, or falsely hope that you are saved already, no wonder you don't seriously seek conversion. You are like many people who have cancer. They hope there is no danger, or they hope it will go away, or they hope that some medical treatment or alternate therapy will cure them – until they have no hope in the end, and finally give up all hope whether they want to or not. This is also the way that many people treat their souls. They know that something is wrong with them, but they hope that God will not condemn them, or they hope to be converted later, or they hope that their prayers and beliefs will save their souls – and they hold onto these false hopes until they see it is too late – and then they die without any hope at all.

> "When a wicked man dieth, his expectation shall perish: and the hope of unjust men perisheth" (Proverbs 11:7).

> "The eyes of the wicked shall fail, and they shall not escape, and their hope shall be as the giving up of the ghost" (Job 11:20).

There is hardly any greater obstacle to conversion than the false hopes of sinners, who think they are converted when they are not, or hope to be saved when they have no reason for such hope.

If you didn't have these false hopes you would be in despair – and might soon be converted.

You must give up all hope of being saved without conversion. You will not find Heaven on the road to Hell. Until strong despair fills your heart, you cannot expect to experience true conversion. You will not give up your sinful pleasures, and go through the difficulties of conversion, as long as you think you can be saved some other way. False hopes keep your heart from breaking, although it ***must*** be broken over your sins.

107

If you *knew* that you must be either converted or condemned, and had no hope of being saved unless you were converted, you would pray hard for conversion, listen carefully to every word of the sermons, follow the advice of your pastor, and give up your lost friends. But you have false hopes that you may be saved the way you are – and so you don't seek conversion strongly enough. Do not be satisfied with saying, "I hope I will be saved." Seek Christ until you find Him (Jeremiah 29:13; Luke 13:24).

The next hindrance to conversion is counterfeit grace, or half-conversion, which does not really change the soul, but only strengthens the false hopes I have mentioned. The person who has a "half-conversion" feels some misery over his sin, gives up lost friends, gives up some former sins, and seems to be converted. He may even think he knows the date, the time, and the sermon that were the means of his "conversion." He may remember a great change in himself and think it was a saving change, and yet only have experienced the superficial convictions and feelings which many lost people have felt. This is a frightening state to be in. It quiets your conscience until you awaken in eternal flames. Oh, if you only knew what a terrible thing it is for people to live all their lives thinking they are saved, and then to die and find they are in eternal misery. It would be horrible if this happens to you. "Examine yourselves, whether ye be in the faith" (II Corinthians 13:5). If you do not examine your counterfeit conversion now, you will have countless ages to do it in Hell.

Another hindrance is neglect of the proper education of children. Many are raised with ignorance of the truths of the Bible until they are adults, and are already hardened in evil habits. Some are even taught from childhood to think it is wrong to be a zealous Christian. All they have heard about real Christianity is negative slander. The things that people learn as little children are generally remembered all their lives. If they receive wrong ideas about being saved when they are children it is hard to change them.

If you were trained in ignorance as a child, seek your salvation while you still have time. If your parents deceived you, don't let them damn you to Hell. If your parents kept you in ignorance, don't keep yourself in ignorance. If they trained you to be a lost person, don't keep being a lost person yourself. You have a friend named Jesus, who is far kinder than your parents. He calls you to come to Him and be saved. Listen to Him, even if everyone else in the world is against you. Do not treat your soul as an unimportant thing, like your parents did. Let the love of Jesus draw you to Heaven, instead of the love of your parents drawing you to Hell.

Another hindrance to conversion is fighting against the Holy Spirit. When God would enlighten a sinner, he often is not willing to see. When God would draw a sinner from his evil way of living and thinking, he is often unwilling to be humbled, and fights against the Holy Spirit, and turns away to think about other things. Jesus said to those who rejected Him:

"How often would I have gathered thy children together,
even as a hen gathereth her chickens under her wings,
and ye would not" (Matthew 23:37).

Jesus may say to a sinner, *"How often I showed you a better way, and you would not go the way I showed you. How often I showed you the misery of your way of life, and you would not leave it."* When you fight against Christ and close your eyes because you hate the light, and when you resist the Holy Spirit, is it any wonder that you remain lost?

If you want to be saved, surrender to the Spirit of God. If you refuse His help when He offers it, He may leave you helpless, and be right in doing so. You cannot be converted unless it is done by the Holy Spirit. But you are resisting Him. How impossible conversion is without His help! The person who wants to be healthy will not insult his doctor and drive him away. Be careful how you treat the Spirit of God if you want to be saved!

Another hindrance to conversion is indecision, when people hesitate between Christ and the world of sin. The Bible says:

"A double minded man is unstable in all his ways"
(James 1:8).

Many people are lost because they hesitate. They are convinced that they must be converted or perish, and yet they wait, they hesitate between two opinions. They never give themselves to Christ. They stop to think about it until God gives up on them, or death finds them still hesitating, and unsaved.

If you want to be converted, do not keep wavering. Turn to Christ.

109

> "How long halt [hesitate] ye between two opinions? If the Lord be God, follow him: but if Baal [Satan], then follow him" (I Kings 18:21).

If it is better to be lost for eternity than to leave your sins and turn to Christ, then keep on sinning, and keep the curse of God on yourself. But if it is better to deny yourself, than to suffer the wrath of God, then throw out your sinful practices and turn to Jesus Christ. If it is better to live with sinful friends for a while than to go to Heaven, then keep on being with them. But if it is better to go to Heaven, then why not give up lost friends and come to Christ? How blind a lost person is that he should remain undecided about these things! Why remain undecided whether it is best to go to Heaven, or not? Why remain undecided whether it is best to be damned or not? Why keep on being undecided because you love wickedness? If this is wise, then what is foolish?

Another hindrance is delay. Many people realize that they must be converted or condemned, and yet they put it off. They say, "I will be converted in the future, but not yet." They think they have plenty of time. They are still healthy, and they believe that they still have time to think it over, and study it some more. Because they believe that Christ will receive them whenever they turn to Him, they think it is all right to stay away from Him a little longer. But they may become hardened by the habits of sin. And many are cut off before they turn to Christ. Many thousands of souls are lost forever who once thought they would be converted. And this happened to them because they delayed their conversion. As the lazy man says, "Yet a little sleep, a little slumber" (Proverbs 6:10; 24:33), so the sinner says, "I can sin a little longer," until he has sinned beyond the possibility of conversion, and has provoked God to leave him. And so he must go to Hell because he waited too long.

Think, sinner, that conversion is not something you should put off. Should a wise person stay under the wrath of God even one more day? The fact that you put off your conversion until the future shows that your heart is deceitful, and that you are not really willing to be converted. Those who are not willing to leave their sin today will probably never leave it, if they can figure out how to keep it. Those who love God would rather be reconciled to Him today than tomorrow.

If you knew who God was, you would not put off your conversion to Him. If you knew how glorious Heaven is, which He offers, you would not put off being sure of going there any longer. If you saw what sin is, and its horrible effects, you would quickly turn from it to Jesus Christ. *If you had poisonous snakes in your shirt, wouldn't you grab them and throw them out? Or would you leave them wiggling in your shirt until tomorrow? You would certainly shake them from you now!* Sinner, how long will you delay? Will you put off conversion until death takes ahold of you, and you drop into Hell? God has not promised that He will offer you salvation any longer, if you continue to resist Christ. How horrible it will be for you when He rejects you forever and departs from you.

> "Woe also to them when I depart from them!" (Hosea 9:12).

> "Be thou instructed...lest my soul depart from thee; lest I make thee desolate" (Jeremiah 6:8).

When people reject God, and will not listen to His voice, He often gives them up to the lusts of their own hearts, to do whatever they want in a God-forsaken life of sin:

> "But my people would not hearken to my voice; and...would none of me. So I gave them up unto their own hearts' lust: and they walked in their own counsels" (Psalm 81:11-12).

If you had any sense, you would say, "I have treated Christ badly long enough. I am completely ashamed of it, and I will no longer treat Him wrong. I have rejected Christ long enough, and have listened to His enemy the Devil far too long already." *If your heart were awakened to think of your condition, you would run as quickly from your sin to Christ as you would from a burning house, or from a boat sinking under you.* Haven't you rejected Christ long enough, and served Satan long enough, and sinned long enough? Haven't you rejected the converting grace of God long enough? Haven't you done enough to destroy your soul already? Haven't you drunk enough of the deadly poison of sin? Haven't you injured yourself enough by your wickedness? Do you want to harm yourself even more? Will you continue on in a lost condition until you die, and it's too late for you to turn to Christ?

> "To day if ye will hear his voice, Harden not your hearts" (Hebrews 3:7-8).

You may never again have the feelings and impressions that you have right now. Do not put off your conversion to Christ any longer.

CHAPTER TWELVE

HINDRANCES TO CONVERSION –
CONTINUED

"Who did hinder you that ye should not
obey the truth?" (Galatians 5:7).

*Another great obstacle to conversion is not persevering until it
actually occurs.* Usually a preparatory work goes on before real
conversion happens. People have many convictions and troubles in
their minds before they come to Christ. If they valued these
convictions and turmoils, and sought more light than they have, they
would be converted soon. But when they lose the convictions they
once had, and turn back to the sins they once loved, no wonder God
leaves them unconverted.

Some have grown cold and lost their convictions, as though they
never had such feelings. Others have turned back to the cares of this
world, and so the hopeful beginning they had has come to nothing,
and they are in their old condition again, having had a false
conversion which was only partial.

If you are such a sinner, you should "be zealous...and repent"
(Revelation 3:19). Have you turned like a dog to its vomit, and like a
pig to its wallowing in the mud? (II Peter 2:22). Did you look back
after putting your hand to the plough? (Luke 9:62). What reason did
Christ give you to turn from Him? Have you found that Satan is a
better master, and that living in sin is the best way? The thought of
eternal life was very important to you at one time, but not now. Has
God become unimportant also? Has Christ become unimportant?
Are you now able to resist God's anger and punishment? Remember
that God has said if you draw back, He will have no pleasure in you
(Hebrews 10:38). Those who draw back will find that they go to
Hell. They "backslid" because they never fully entered salvation in
the first place. They had a "partial conversion," not the full and real
experience of it. They drew back into perdition instead of believing
to the saving of their souls (Hebrews 10:39). There is no one more

miserable than a person who once began to seek conversion but went back to sin. The end of such people is worse than their beginning (II Peter 2:20-21). It will be sad to see people who had false conversions condemned to Hell at the Last Judgment.

In the name of God, I warn every one who has gone back to sin to think about your soul. Oh, be awakened from your foolishness, come back and do the first works. Repent and turn fully to Jesus Christ. Oh, do not sleep on until Hell awakens you!

The next hindrance to conversion is misunderstanding the Scriptures, and wrong thinking about the ways of God. If error remains in your mind, it will keep saving grace out of your heart. I will give several ways this can happen.

1. *Some do not know what true conversion is.* Therefore they think they have it when they don't, and as a result they don't look for it. They think conversion is merely giving up some big sins, and doing some outward service to God, and doing good deeds toward others, and this makes them think they have true conversion, because they have turned away from some evil things. But these people should realize that conversion is more than this. It is a strong turning from the world and from carnal desires, and the devotion of yourself completely to Jesus Christ. No matter how zealous you are, or how strict you are, this is no proof of real conversion, if you are not united with Christ.

2. *Some don't think that there is any such thing as conversion.* The reason they think this is because they have not had it happen to them, and therefore they think no one else has experienced it. They think that those who say they are converted are only talking, and have never really gone through it. But these people should understand that it is a terrible thing to contradict the Bible, God's Word. And it is wrong to contradict the experience of those who are truly Christians. They should also understand that they are against conversion because they are so sinful themselves. Since God's Word speaks of saving people, and purifying a peculiar people for Himself who want to live the Christian life

(Titus 2:14), how dare they say that there is no such thing as conversion? Since Christ died to purchase their conversion and the Holy Spirit has been sent to produce it, how can they say there is no such thing? Would the Bible, and the preachers, and the churches work for your conversion if such a thing were not possible? If you refuse to believe the Bible and the experience of those who have already been converted, you will be forced to see the truth at the Last Judgment, and you will be ashamed on that day for rejecting conversion when you could have had it.

3. ***Others think that holiness is not needed, and that it is not necessary to make salvation our main concern.*** They think that too much concern about conversion causes people to be strange and unbalanced mentally.

Although I have already answered this objection, yet the subject comes up again, and I will reply to it.

    (1) Tell me, do you think God has told us to do something that is not necessary? Are you saying that you are smarter than God? Do you dare to say that He requires you to do more than is necessary?

    (2) Then I ask, is it wrong for the Bible to call you to holiness? Jesus said, "Lay not up for yourselves treasures upon earth; but lay up for yourselves treasures in heaven. Seek ye first the kingdom of God and his righteousness" (Matthew 6:33). "The kingdom of heaven suffereth violence, and the violent take it by force" (Matthew 11:12). "Strive to enter in at the strait gate: for many, I say unto you, will seek to enter in, and shall not be able" (Luke 13:24). "Labour not for the meat which perisheth, but for that meat which endureth unto everlasting life" (John 6:27). "What

manner of persons ought ye to be in all holy conversation and godliness"? (II Peter 3:11). A hundred more Scriptures could be mentioned to show you that you should have great concern about your salvation. God Himself is the one who said so. And who is more likely to be right, you or God? You hardly know good from evil, and do you think you are wiser than God?

(3) Do you think that a person can do too much to gain Heaven? Is a person fit to see God in Heaven if he thinks Heaven is not worth the greatest efforts? Do you think that God and Heaven are so unimportant that the eternal enjoyment of them is not worth striving for? (Luke 13:23-24).

(4) Do you think anyone who got to Heaven was ever sorry he spent so much effort to get there? If you could speak to someone who is already in Heaven, and ask him, "Who is wiser, the person who does all he can to be converted, or the one who says, 'Why be so worried about it?'" Which side do you think a wise man would take?

(5) Did Christ, or the Apostles, or any real Christian, think like you? Read in the Bible whether they thought that salvation was the most important thing in life. The Christians in Bible times never felt they had enough grace, but always wanted more. They never felt that they were holy enough, but they always wanted more holiness, they always wanted to be better than they were. And do you think that you are wiser than they were? Do you think that the Apostles or early Christians didn't

know what they were doing when they sought for salvation and holiness so strongly?

(6) What is it that you think is too hard to do to get to Heaven? Do you know what you are talking about? Being a real Christian is the only joyful life anyone can have on earth. What is holiness? It is living in the love of God and in the joy of the Holy Spirit, and the great hope of life to come, and daily communion with God, and in attending church with joy, to hear of God's love, and the promise of Heaven, and the forgiveness of sins. And do you think this is a hard way to live? Is it hard work to eat and drink when you are hungry and thirsty, or to love your closest friend and be with Him? If you say "no," then why should you feel that it's too hard to live in the love of God, and work for Him in the local church?

(7) Isn't it a sure sign of an unconverted heart if you think working for God is too hard? A man who hates his wife and loves prostitutes will say, "I cannot love her, or live with her." But if he truly loved her, he would not think that way at all. And if you didn't really reject God, you wouldn't think it's too hard to live in a loving relationship with Him, and be with Him as much as possible.

(8) Do you want to go to Heaven or not? If not, remember that it is you who made the choice to be shut out. If you want to go to Heaven, then don't you realize that all the work you do there will be much more than what you are called to do on earth? Will

117

you think that Heaven itself is too hard a place, and that praising God there is too difficult? If not, how dare you say that a far smaller amount of service to Him in this life is too much? If you are tired of such a small amount of service here, in the local church, how tired would you be in Heaven?

(9) I will ask you one more question. Do you think the trouble it causes to live a holy Christian life is greater than the trouble you will have in Hell? If you don't, shouldn't you choose the lesser to escape the greater? If you don't have enough love for God to make you serve Him, you should at least have enough love for yourself to make you fear God's everlasting wrath. *Remember, you must go through the pain of living a holy Christian life, or else you must suffer everlasting torment in Hell. Which will you choose?*

4. *Another error people make is thinking that their prayers and good works will make up for their sins and cause them to be acceptable to God.* They think if their "goodness" won't save them there is nothing else they can do. The truth is that they don't see the selfish evil of their good works. And they don't see the sinfulness of their own natures. They also do not truly see their need for Christ or a thorough change of their condition, so they can be made the justified sons and daughters of God. They think they can live sinful lives and make up for it by praying, and doing "good" things.

They do not see that their good works always come from selfish motives, and that such good works themselves need to be forgiven. Even if your good deeds were perfectly good, they could not atone for the

118

sins you committed in the past. *Forgiveness of sin can only come through the Blood of Christ. It is sad to hear people talk about their commitments and prayers while they make no mention of the Blood of the Redeemer, nor feel the need of it. We hear countless people give "testimonies" that don't even mention the Blood of Christ, and say little about what Christ has done for them, or how much they owe Him.*

It is not fixing up your life that saves you. You must be made wholly new. "If any man be in Christ, he is a new creature; old things are passed away; behold, all things are become new" (II Corinthians 5:17). It is not giving up certain sins or saying a "sinner's prayer" which saves you. You must have a new heart, new motives, and a new life. The main motive of your life must be new.

5. *Another error that hinders conversion is the misunderstanding of Scriptures which seem to promise salvation for doing some particular thing.* "Whosoever believeth in him should not perish," therefore they think they are saved because they believe in Him mentally. Even though they have no holiness of life, they believe this Scripture has promised them salvation. They misunderstand it. Another Scripture which is often misunderstood is "Whosoever shall call upon the name of the Lord shall be saved." Therefore they say, "I have called on the name of the Lord, so I am saved" – even though they are not converted. To these people I have several things to say:

> (1) You don't know what you are talking about. You are deceived by words that you don't understand in the whole context of Scripture. Sin is the evil which Christ saves you from, and conversion is the saving work He does in you. How can you say you believe, and therefore do not need to be converted? How can you say, "I believe in Christ to

save me from my sins," and yet you go on committing those sins? *These are the ideas self-conceited people use to delude themselves and others. How can Christ save you, if you will not be converted from serving sin to serving God?*

(2) Is it a wise argument to say that you can believe in Jesus without being converted? It is as foolish as saying that you can have sunshine, and yet see without its light. *There is no such thing as true faith without conversion.*

(3) Where true faith in Christ is, all other saving graces accompany it; there is repentance, hope, love, humility, and a Heavenly way of thinking. *So, saving faith cannot be separated from any of these. It is false to say it can be.*

If you want to be converted, humbly submit to the Word of God, and to the instruction of those men of God whom He has given to teach you. What unreasonable pride those people have who reject the counsel of ministers, where God Himself leads them in His Word. Are these ministers not likely to know more than you, who have studied these subjects all their lives? Talk with them and see whether they have more knowledge of conversion than you. Consider how foolish you are when you proudly argue against the necessity of conversion and a holy life. Are you wiser than your teachers, whom God has sent to convert you? Many people who know hardly anything about Christianity are yet so proud that they reject the instruction of the wisest preachers.

I tell you that the conviction of God's judgments will bring you down to ruin before long. The day is coming when your pride will humble you – either in conversion or in eternal damnation. Listen while there is still time, otherwise you will "mourn at the last, when thy flesh and thy body are consumed; and say, How have I hated instruction, and my heart despised reproof; and have not obeyed the voice of my teachers, nor inclined mine ear to them that instructed me" (Proverbs 5:11-13). *If you think you're too smart to learn, then you're too dumb to be saved.*

The last hindrance to conversion that I will mention is rebellious obstinacy. When people have resisted God's grace for a long time, they are often given over to reprobation, and they grow so hardened they can never be saved. They say, "I will not be converted." They will not seek holiness, nor deny their sin, nor give up the world of sin, nor devote themselves to a heavenly life in the local church. They become so hardened that they don't believe it is necessary to be converted, and they can never be changed from this rebelliousness. This desperate state of rebellion is Satan's strongest hold on them, and he will bind them in sin forever.

What can I say to you to get you to give up this hindrance? When your heart is so corrupted and rebellious, whatever I say will be rejected by you. All I can do is ask you to go back over what I have written, and tell you to think deeply about what I have already said. But I have little hope of convincing many of you. Because so many are in this horrible condition, I am forced to end this book with great sadness.

Conclusion

I know that both you and I will soon appear before God, to give a strict account of our lives. And if I have not taught you with sincerity, with a true desire for the salvation of your soul, how can I stand before the Lord?

If you have read this book and yet come to the Last Judgment in an unconverted state, what will you be able to give as an excuse? Or how will you escape the threats of damnation? I hope I will meet some of you in Heaven, and that you will be able to say that this book helped you to be converted. But I am afraid that I will see great numbers of you in an unconverted state. This makes me want to sit down and weep, now that I have finished this book.

Have I written all this to condemn you at the Last Judgment? I know that every soul who has read this book and rejected it will pass out of his body in an unconverted state. I know that every one of you will be forever in Hell. And I know that you have been warned so often that you are left without excuse, and will therefore have a double condemnation, because now it is your rebellion which keeps you from true conversion.

If you will look over the directions I have given you, and begin to practice them, you will be converted. If not, what hope do you have? Particularly, read the Scriptures daily, leave your sinful friends behind, get into a Bible-believing church among those who fear the Lord, and take all opportunities to listen to the sermons, and counsel with preachers who do not practice superficial "decisionism."

I have delivered my message, and I hope God will not require your blood at my hands. Remember that I told you there is no salvation without conversion. I showed you the reasonableness of the offers of God, and that if you are not converted, it will be because you would not come to Christ, and what a torment it will be everlastingly to your conscience to think that you stubbornly destroyed yourself, that you deliberately refused salvation, and that you could have been in Heaven if you had not obstinately rejected real conversion through Christ. I say, what a tormenting thought this will be to you eternally, you cannot possibly know now, in this life. But in eternity you will feel the horror of it, if true conversion does not lead you to Christ and Heaven. It is my prayer that what I have written will lead you to a real conversion. As long as I have life and strength, this will continue to be my earnest prayer.

> "I preach as never sure to preach again,
> and as a dying man to dying men"
> – Richard Baxter.
> AD 1657

AFTERWORD —
THREE REPRINTED BOOKS THAT WILL
HELP PASTORS RESTORE OUR CHURCHES

by Dr. R. L. Hymers, Jr.

> The fact is that we are not today producing saints. We are making converts to an effete type of Christianity that bears little resemblance to that of the New Testament. The average so-called Bible Christian in our times is but a parody on true sainthood. Yet we put millions of dollars behind movements to perpetuate this degenerate form of religion and attack the man who dares to challenge the wisdom of it...
> – A. W. Tozer,
> *Of God and Men*,
> Christian Publications, 1960, p. 13.

I hope this updated version of Richard Baxter's *Treatise on Conversion* has been a blessing. You probably noticed how different his message was from that of most modern evangelicals. A great change in beliefs about conversion began under the ministry of Charles G. Finney (1792-1875). Before Finney, all Protestants and Baptists were in basic agreement with Baxter's views. But Finney rejected the depravity of man and the Blood Atonement of Christ (see *Today's Apostasy* by R. L. Hymers, Jr. and Christopher Cagan, Hearthstone Publishing, 1999). Finney also promoted a superficial form of decisionism, which was generally accepted by the end of the nineteenth century, and virtually overturned the old methods of evangelism in the twentieth century. *The change has been so overwhelming that most preachers in our day are not even aware that there was once a different and more effective way of leading the lost to Christ.*

As a result, the *vast majority* of preachers are decisionists today, whether they know it or not. Merely eliminating the invitation does not cure decisionism. Changing from classical Arminianism to Calvinism does not cure it either, in my opinion. Most evangelicals in America are neither Arminian nor Calvinist anyway. Most of them

123

are practicing Pelagians, which means they have followed Finney in his view that man is not wholly ruined by the Fall. If man is not totally depraved, then he can do something to save himself, such as going forward, saying a "sinner's prayer," believing a few Bible verses or some other superficial human act which in fact, if not in word, leaves Jesus Christ and His Blood out of the central equation. This is why Jesus forgiving sin through His Blood atonement is seldom the main theme of "personal testimonies" today. People talk about what *they* have done, rather than what *Christ* has done for them. Of course, these multitudes are still lost.

Decisionist pastors practice superficial counselling, to "get it over with" as quickly as possible. Such men can do the lost little good, I know. A lost person should seek out the rare preacher who will take much time to do what Baxter and all the old preachers did – by having many counselling sessions with you, asking you probing questions. These must be preachers who are not in a hurry to have you make a superficial commitment, or have you say a quick "sinner's prayer" and let it go at that.

To overcome these ruinous methods of decisionism, there must be a return to the Biblical view of the total depravity of man, which is perfectly acceptable to classical Arminians as well as Calvinists. *We must once again realize that people are not only incapable of saving themselves, but they are also inwardly opposed to God. There are no exceptions to this in the Bible* (cf. Romans 3:9-20; Ephesians 2:1-5; Ephesians 4:18). That is why a person can only be saved when God is drawing him to Jesus Christ, who said:

> "No man can come to me, except the Father which hath
> sent me draw him, and I will raise him up at the last
> day" (John 6:44).

The mind of the Pelagianist runs quickly away from this verse, without ever dealing with the actual meaning of Christ's words. But heretics cannot be corrected by Scripture as a rule.

During the time when God is drawing sinners to Jesus, the ministry of preachers is crucial. The Bible tells us that pastors are given by Christ for the purpose of evangelism as well as teaching (cf. Ephesians 4:7-16), including the "increase of the body" (Ephesians 4:16). What evangelical pastor knows very much about the inner workings of Satan, and the twisted deceptions of sinners' hearts? If this is true of them, how can they lead people out of the quagmire of depraved confusion?

> "The heart is deceitful above all things, and desperately wicked: who can know it?" (Jeremiah 17:9).

> "For from within, out of the heart of man, proceed evil thoughts, adulteries, fornications, murders, thefts, covetousness, wickedness, deceit, lasciviousness, an evil eye, blasphemy, pride, foolishness: All these evil things come from within, and defile the man" (Mark 7:21-23).

Decisionism has robbed most evangelical pastors of Biblical discernment, so that virtually *any* "decision" is accepted as a salvation experience, whether the sinner has actually been united with the risen Christ or not.

The only remedy for this deplorable condition in the churches is for pastors to take charge of counselling inquirers themselves. This delicate work simply cannot be delegated to others without more floods of unconverted people streaming into the churches. Even associate pastors should not have this work delegated to them. No one but the pastor should deal with the lost, particularly during the first several years that this method is adopted in a church. If preachers don't deliver the babies most of them will be still-born.

One man who built a large church in the South, without counselling people himself, recently told me that this proves pastoral counselling is unnecessary. My reply is this: the Mormons build even bigger churches than his! They don't counsel the lost as we have suggested either! Thus, gathering large crowds of unsaved people into a church building proves nothing!

Dr. Tom Nettles, a conservative professor at Southern Baptist Theological Seminary, Louisville, Kentucky, has said that "contemporary pastors...have few if any models of pastors who understand the 'work of evangelism'" (*A Pastor's Sketches* by Dr. I. S. Spencer, back cover).

Two books are recommended to guide preachers back to the old paths of soul winning, before Finney's methods ruined evangelism. The first book is titled *Revival Sketches and Manual*, by Dr. Heman Humphrey, first published in 1859 by the American Tract Society. It has been reprinted by Sprinkle Publications, P.O. Box 1094, Harrisburg, Virginia 22801. Telephone (540)434-8840 to order it.

Pages 327 through 367 of Dr. Humphrey's book should be studied by every pastor in America and Great Britain. This section is titled "Revival Conversations Between a Pastor and Inquirers." *Preacher, your entire ministry could be changed forever by reading these forty pages! It is probably not like anything you have ever read on soul-winning!* In his foreword to the book, Baptist pastor Randy H. Rice, Sr. says of Dr. Humphrey:

> He had a deep desire for the salvation of souls and for the revival of God's cause in the world...Reading this volume has put such a desire in me for these matters which are at the heart of our business in the Kingdom of God. My prayer is that God will use it in a similar manner in the lives of many others as well" (ibid., p. xiii).

I am certain that pages 327 to 367 of Dr. Heman Humphrey's book will do just that for any pastor who orders it, reads it, and puts it into practice. These pages show the old way that pastors counselled the lost, all but forgotten in this age of apostasy.

The second book we recommend is titled *A Pastor's Sketches* by Dr. I. S. Spencer, written in 1850 and republished in 2001 by Solid Ground Christian Books, P.O. Box 660132, Vestavia Hills, Alabama 35266. Telephone (205)978-9469 to order it. This book presents pastoral interviews with the lost, and is quite similar to Dr. Humphrey's book, but deals with pastoral counselling for a full 277 pages. Spencer's book is an exciting reproduction of his interviews with the lost. While I disagree with his view of Baptism, as presented in one brief "sketch," I heartily recommend the rest of the book to any preacher who is truly seeking the old way of revival counselling, as it was once done by Baptist and Protestant pastors throughout the world before Finney's decisionism ruined the churches.

Every preacher should have these two books in his library, and should review them constantly. I hope you don't buy one without the other. Please get them both, because they complement each other. *I do not believe that we will ever again experience a great general revival unless there is a return to the type of pastoral counselling presented by these two men of the past.*

I also recommend that you get a copy of *Today's Apostasy* (Hearthstone, 1999) by Dr. Christopher Cagan and myself. On pages

131 to 167 we deal specifically with how to interview the lost in a modern pastoral setting. Phone (818)352-0452 to order it.

Richard Baxter, who wrote the book you just read back in 1657, used exactly the same methods as Dr. Humphrey and Dr. Spencer (cf. *The Reformed Pastor* by Richard Baxter, Banner of Truth Trust, 1999, reprint of the 1656 edition).

But the kind of counselling advocated by Spencer, Humphrey, and Baxter will do little good unless it follows old-fashioned "law before gospel," Hell-fire and Blood preaching. A growing number of preachers are interested in "tacking on" the counselling of Spencer, Humphrey, and Baxter without first *preaching* like they did! *Counselling sessions after a typical dry-as-dust "expository sermon" will not produce conversions very often – if ever.* For an example of how to preach in a way that will make Spencer's and Humphrey's counselling of benefit, buy a copy of *Sermons From the Second Great Awakening* by Dr. Asahel Nettleton. These are the actual sermons of Nettleton, the greatest American evangelist of all time in my opinion. He counselled just as Humphrey, Spencer, and Baxter did. By reading his sermons, you will see how you must preach before this kind of counselling will do much good. Order Nettleton's book of sermons by phoning (515)292-9594, or by writing to International Outreach at P.O. Box 1286, Ames, Iowa 50014.

Every preacher should have the book of Nettleton's sermons, and the two corresponding books on counselling by Spencer and Humphrey. These three books will take you back to the revival days of the Second Great Awakening, before Charles G. Finney ruined evangelism. I believe that true revival could be sent again by God if some of our preachers had the courage to go back to olden times, preach to the lost like Nettleton, Humphrey, Spencer, and Baxter, and then counsel them as these men did, who lived in the glory days of true revival.

It is my prayer that God will bless you as you read these books. May you experience the reality of true conversions in your church by going back to the old Puritan pattern of evangelism.

Our website is at www.rlhymersjr.com. It features word-for-word sermons, as given each Sunday in our church, the Fundamentalist Baptist Tabernacle, located in the heart of downtown Los Angeles.